W9-CBA-968

PET PROJECTS
THE ANIMAL KNITS BIBLE

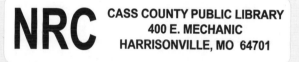
NRC CASS COUNTY PUBLIC LIBRARY
400 E. MECHANIC
HARRISONVILLE, MO 64701

SALLY MUIR & JOANNA OSBORNE

0 0022 0393707 9

PET PROJECTS

THE ANIMAL KNITS BIBLE

SALLY MUIR & JOANNA OSBORNE

PHOTOGRAPHY BY DIANA MILLER

QUADRILLE

The Taunton Press
Inspiration for hands-on living®

The Taunton Press, Inc.,
63 South Main Street, PO Box 5506, Newtown, CT 06470-5506
email: tp@taunton.com

First published in 2007 by **Quadrille Publishing Limited**
Alhambra House, 27–31 Charing Cross Road, London WC2H 0LS

Editorial Director Jane O'Shea
Creative Director Helen Lewis
Project Editor Laura Herring
Designer Katherine Case
Editor and Pattern Checker Sally Harding
Pattern Checker Marilyn Wilson
Photographer Diana Miller
Photographer's Assistant Danielle Wood
Production Vincent Smith, Funsho Asemota

Text © 2007 Sally Muir and Joanna Osborne
Photography © 2007 Diana Miller
Design and layout © 2007 Quadrille Publishing Limited

All rights reserved. No part of this book may be reproduced, stored in a retrieval
system, or transmitted in any form or by any means, electronic, electrostatic, magnetic
tape, mechanical, photocopying, recording, or otherwise, without the prior permission
in writing of the publisher.

While every effort has been made to ensure the safety and comfort of the animals
who might use the projects in this book, the authors and publisher cannot accept
responsibility for any illness or accident arising from the use of these projects.

Library of Congres Cataloging-in-Publication data

Muir, Sally.
  Pet projects : the animal knits bible / Sally Muir and Joanna Osborne.
      p. cm.
  Includes bibliographical references and index.
  ISBN 978-1-60085-127-8 (alk. paper)
  1. Knitting—Patterns. 2. Pet supplies. I. Osborne, Joanna. II. Title.
  TT825.M785 2009
  746.43'2041—dc22

                              2008032422

Printed in China

CONTENTS

INTRODUCTION

At last you can lavish your affection and skill on the pet that you love. **Pet Projects** includes an extensive range of designs for almost every pet imaginable: hamsters, cats, horses, goldfish, birds, dogs, tortoises, and more. What cat wouldn't yearn for a mouse mat to lounge on? What fourteen-year-old would not want to knit their horse a personalized blanket? Who wouldn't want to make a sophisticated and stylish tent for their tortoise to winter in, or a balaclava to protect their dog's ears from the misery of fireworks? Without spending a fortune, you can now adorn and accessorize your pet, and keep him up to date with fashion.

Our patterns range from simple designs, which can be knitted by the ten-year-old beginner for her new kitten, to more complicated patterns, like the wire bird feeder, for the experienced knitter in search of an exciting challenge. The designs are meant to be practical as well as chic—they aren't intended just for dressing up your pet. And we intend these patterns to be adaptable. If you don't have a dog but like the look of the party dog collars, then why not make one for your ferret? If your pot-bellied pig would like to lounge on a dog beanbag, why not? As well as providing patterns that you can follow, we would like you to use this book as a basis to invent accessories to suit the particular foibles of your own individual pet. Use it as a source of ideas and don't feel you have to slavishly follow each pattern. We would like you to change the colors or shapes, or customize it in any way you like. Pets come in a vast array of sizes and shapes, so use these ideas to make your unique pet its own personalized knitted accessory. Finally, even if you don't have an animal of your own, we wouldn't want you to feel discriminated against: you can still award yourself a rosette, make a slightly larger beanbag or even knit your very own easy-care companion from our selection of knitted pets.

KNITTING BASICS

KNITTING FOR PETS

YARN SPECIFICS

The accessories in this book have been designed using Rowan and Jaeger Yarns, which are widely available throughout the United States, Europe, and over the Internet. Visit www.knitrowan.com where you will find a full range of yarns, colors, and suppliers (and see pages 142–143). If you are a beginner, you can go to a local yarn store where the helpful staff will give you all the assistance you need to track down yarns.

The majority of these pet accessories are knitted in double-knitting-weight wool yarns. If you decide to use a yarn other than the specified yarn, do remember to knit a 4in (10cm) square to check the gauge and then adjust the needle size accordingly.

The number of yards (meters) per 1¾oz (50g) ball varies from yarn to yarn, so when using a substitute yarn, be sure to calculate the number of balls you need by the number of yards (meters) rather than by weight.

Some of the designs use small amounts of several colors. These give you the opportunity to use up leftover yarns. Before beginning, however, check the yarn descriptions on page 142 to make sure that your leftovers are a good match in thickness to the main color you are using.

GAUGE

Working your knitting to the correct size can be important, especially for dog coats, so be sure to knit a gauge swatch. Count the number of stitches and rows to 4in (10cm) on your swatch. If your swatch has more rows or stitches than the number specified, then use knitting needles that are one size larger, and if it has fewer stitches or rows, then try one size smaller needles. Getting the number of stitches to 4in (10cm) right is more important than the number of rows, as length is generally determined by merely knitting to a specified length in inches (centimeters).

Working a gauge swatch sounds tedious, but it is definitely worth the time it takes, particularly if the design comes in various sizes. The swatch also gives you a chance to see how the yarn and stitch pattern knit up. Keep these swatches, and once you have collected about 20, sew them together into a blanket for your pet (see the Horse Blanket on page 54 for an example of knitted patchwork).

DOG COAT SIZES

The dog coat patterns are written for five sizes. But dogs do vary enormously in size. Here are the measurements on which we based most of our dog coats:

	Chest	Body length	Collar
Extra small	12in/30.5cm	12in/30.5cm	10in/25.5cm
Small	16in/40.5cm	14in/35.5cm	11in/27.5cm
Medium	20in/50.5cm	18in/45.5cm	13in/33cm
Large	24in/61cm	22in/56cm	15in/38cm
Extra large	26in/66cm	24in/61cm	17in/43cm

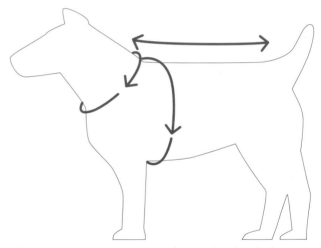

When you are measuring your dog to decide which size to knit, the most important measurement is around the widest part of the dog's chest, just behind the front legs, followed by the collar size and then the body length. For example, if your dog has a medium-sized rib cage, a small neck, and a long back, it is best to opt for Medium.

It is very easy to shorten or lengthen a dog coat, and the best place is mentioned in the individual patterns.

PROTECT YOUR PETS

The most essential thing to remember when knitting for your pets is to make sure that all beads and buttons are securely sewn on—you don't want your animals to swallow them.

Follow these knitting instructions to learn how to knit. With these basics you can make all of the easy and intermediate patterns in this book. Or, best of all, ask an experienced knitter to show you how to knit—it is so much easier to learn when shown first hand.

For more extensive techniques, look on the Internet (try www.knitting-and-crochet-guild.org.uk or www.angelyarns.com).

CASTING ON

There are several ways of casting on, but this is the method that we prefer. It gives a more elastic edge than other techniques, which is useful when the cast-on row is followed by a garter stitch or stockinette stitch fabric. Start with a slip knot—this forms the first loop of the cast-on stitches.

The slip knot

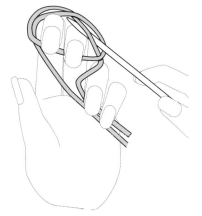

1 Wind the yarn twice around two fingers.

2 Using a knitting needle, pull the back loop through the front one to form a loop on the needle. Pull the yarn ends to tighten the loop on the needle.

The thumb cast-on

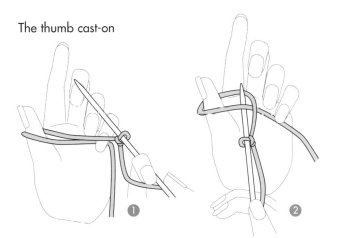

1 Make a slip knot about 39in (1 meter) from the end of the yarn. (You can alter this length in future according to the number of stitches needed.) Holding the knitting needle with the slip knot in your right hand, wind the loose end of yarn around your left thumb from front to back as shown (and leave the ball end of the yarn hanging for the time being).
2 Insert the needle under the loop on your thumb as shown.

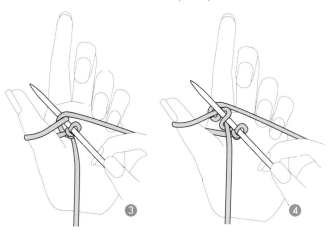

3 Wrap the yarn coming from the ball around the tip of the needle as shown.
4 Draw the yarn around the needle through the loop on the thumb to form a stitch. To create even stitches, tighten the cast-on loop by removing your left thumb close to the right needle. Continue in this way until you have the required number of cast-on stitches.

THE KNIT STITCH

1 Hold the needle with the cast-on stitches in your left hand and the yarn coming from the ball at the back of the work. Insert the tip of the right-hand needle from left to right into the front of the first stitch on the left-hand needle.
2 Wrap the yarn over the right-hand needle as shown.

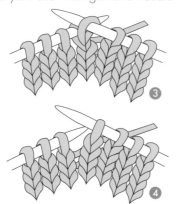

3 Draw the yarn wrapped around the right-hand needle through the stitch on the left-hand needle to make a new stitch on the right-hand needle. Slip the original stitch off the left-hand needle.
4 Continue in this way until all the stitches on the left-hand needle have been knitted and transferred onto the right-hand needle. The first row has been completed.

THE PURL STITCH

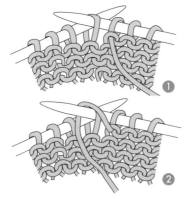

1 Hold the needle with the cast-on stitches on in your left hand and the yarn coming from the ball at the front of the work. Insert the tip of the right-hand needle from right to left into the front of the first stitch on the left-hand needle.
2 Wrap the yarn over the right-hand needle as shown.

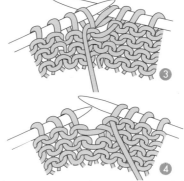

3 Draw the yarn wrapped around the right-hand needle through the stitch on the left-hand needle to make a new stitch on the right-hand needle. Slip the original stitch off the left-hand needle.
4 Continue in this way until all the stitches on the left-hand needle have been knitted and transferred onto the right-hand needle.

BASIC STITCH PATTERNS

The basic stitch patterns in knitting are garter stitch, stockinette stitch, reverse stockinette stitch, ribbing, and seed stitch. They are all formed by simple combinations of knit and purl stitches.

Garter stitch
If every row is worked in knit stitches, garter stitch is formed. Garter stitch fabric has a bumpy appearance. It has more rows per inch (centimeter) than stockinette stitch and is reversible.

Stockinette stitch
Stockinette stitch is formed by working a row of knit stitches and a row of purl stitches alternately. The smooth side (the knit-stitch side) is the right side.

Reverse stockinette stitch
Reverse stockinette stitch is formed in exactly the same way as stockinette stitch, but the knobbly side (the purl-stitch side) is the right side.

Ribbing
Ribbing is an elastic knitted fabric generally used for borders. Work alternate knit and purl stitches across the row. On the following rows all the knit stitches are knit and all the purl stitches purled to create vertical ridges.

Seed stitch

Like ribbing, seed stitch is often used for borders on knitting, but it has less elasticity. It is formed by working one knit stitch and one purl stitch alternately across the first row, then on following rows, purling each knit stitch and knitting each purl stitch.

LOOPY STITCH

There are many techniques for creating loop stitches in knitting, but this is the method used for the toy Guinea Pig's coat (see page 122). It creates secure loops approximately ³/₄in (2cm) long on the right side of the knitting.

You can work as many or as few rows as you wish in garter stitch between the loop rows, but always work the loop stitches at the back of the work on a wrong side row.

Begin the row by inserting the tip of the right needle knitwise into the first stitch on the left needle. Place the first finger of the left hand behind the stitch and wrap the yarn around the finger and the tip of right needle as shown, then knit the stitch without dropping it from the left needle. Keeping the finger inside the yarn wrap, insert the tip of the left needle from right to left through the front of the stitch just made (on the right needle) and slip this stitch back onto the left needle. Knit the slipped stitch and the next stitch on the left needle together through the back of the loops (k2tog tbl). Now slide the finger out of the loop. This completes the first loop stitch. Work every stitch in the same way to the end of the row.

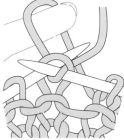

BINDING OFF

When your knitting is finished, you bind off the remaining stitches. It is important to always work the stitches in the pattern stitch used. For example, if the bind-off row follows a purl row in a stockinette stitch fabric, work a knitwise bind-off as shown below.

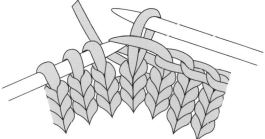

1   For a knitwise bind-off, begin by knitting the first two stitches. Then using the left-hand needle, lift the first stitch over the second stitch and drop it off the right-hand needle. Knit the next stitch and repeat.

2   Continue to do this until one stitch remains on the right-hand needle. Slip this remaining stitch off the needle, break off the yarn, pass the yarn end through the loop, and pull tightly to secure.

For a purlwise bind-off, repeat as above but working in purl stitches.

INCREASING

When knitting some of the accessories in this book, you may need to use one of these two increasing methods. Each one has a particular purpose.

Working into the front and back of a stitch
(known as "inc 1")
This increase is usually used when a single increase is needed at the beginning and the end of a row.

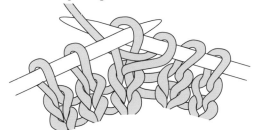

Knit into the stitch, and before slipping it off the left-hand needle, knit into the back of the same stitch as shown to make an extra stitch.

Yarn over
(known as "yo")
This increase method is used in lace stitch patterns (and for buttonholes) because it creates a visible hole in the knitted fabric.

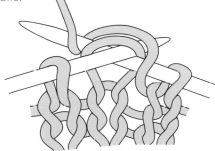

On a knit row, bring the yarn to the front of the work between the two needles, then take it over the right-hand needle to the back of the work and knit the next stitch in the usual way as shown. This creates an extra loop on the right-hand needle.

DECREASING

The two methods for decreasing used in this book are the simple decrease and the slip-stitch decrease.

Simple decrease
(known as "k2tog" or "p2tog")

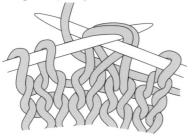

On a knit row, insert the right-hand needle into two stitches and knit them together as one stitch as shown. On a purl row, purl the two stitches together.

Slip-stitch decrease
(known as "sl 1, k1, psso")

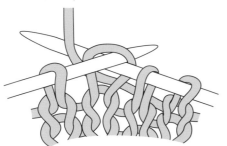

1 Slip the next stitch onto the right-hand needle *(sl 1)*, then knit the next stitch *(k1)*.

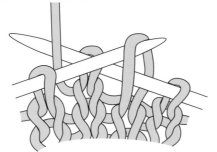

2 Pass the slipped stitch over the knit stitch and let it drop off the right-hand needle *(psso)*.

JOINING IN NEW YARN

If you need to join in a new ball of yarn, it is much easier to start it at the beginning of a new row. If you are knitting stripes, however, do not cut off the yarn every time you change colors. Instead, drop the yarn at the side of the knitting and pick it up again when you need the same color again. (This only works when the stripes have an even number of rows.)

COLOR KNITTING

There are two main techniques for working with more than one color in the same row of knitting—the intarsia technique and the stranding (or Fair Isle) technique.

Intarsia technique

This method is used when knitting individual, large blocks of color. It is best to a use small ball (or long length) for each area of color, otherwise the yarns will easily become tangled.

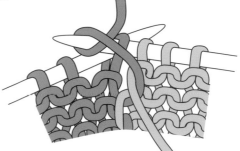

Follow the chart for the color pattern, and when changing to the new color, twist the yarns on the wrong side of the work to prevent holes forming.

When starting a new row, turn the knitting so that the yarns that are hanging from the knitting untwist as much as possible. You may occasionally have to reorganize the yarns at the back of the knitting.

Your work may look a little messy but don't be concerned; once the ends are all sewn in and the work is pressed, it will look very impressive.

Stranding (or Fair Isle) technique

If a pattern is repeated in small blocks of color (no more than 4 stitches) across the entire row, you can use the stranding (or Fair Isle) technique.

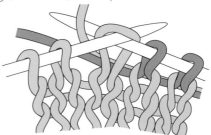

Begin knitting with the first color, then drop this when you introduce the second color. Strand the first color across the back of the second color. When you come to the first color again, take it under the second color to twist the yarns. When you come to the second color again, take it over the first color. The secret of this method is not to pull the strands on the wrong side of the work too tightly, otherwise the work will pucker.

USEFUL HAND STITCHES

MATTRESS STITCH

Mattress stitch is the neatest of all the methods used for sewing seams, and it can be used on any type of seam. As it is worked on the right side of the knitting, it is particularly suited to projects where you need a flat seam and for when you want patterns or stripes to match up— for example, on the Hamster House, the Dog Coats, Cat Cushions, and the Beanbags. For the best finish, work this stitch one stitch in from the edge of the knitting.

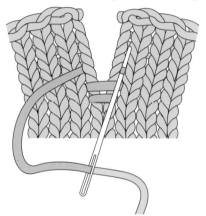

1 With the right sides of the knitting facing you, secure the yarn at the bottom of the seam. Take the yarn to the opposite side, insert the needle under two bars between the first and second stitches and pull the needle through to the front. Repeat this on the opposite side, drawing the edges closely together, but not so tight that the knitting gathers. Continue in the same way.

OVERCAST STITCH/WHIPSTITCH

This stitch can be used if you need a flat seam—for example, on the Horse Blanket and Bird Feeder.

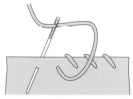

With the right sides together, secure the yarn at the beginning of the seam. Then take the needle over the top of the two edges and from back to front through both layers, close to the edge. Repeat, keeping the stitches slanted at the same angle and evenly spaced. Once pressed this should give a flat seam.

BACKSTITCH

Backstitch is a handy and firm standby stitch for sewing seams on knitting.

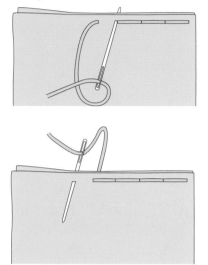

With right sides together, pin and then secure the yarn at the right-hand end. Working over one knitted stitch at a time, bring the needle to the front of the knitting, take it forward and through the knitting to the back. Next, take the needle along one knitted stitch and out to the front, and then return to the end of the first stitch and through to the back. As with learning to knit, the easiest way to learn this is to watch someone else doing it.

BLANKET STITCH

Blanket stitch is used to give a fabric a finished edge—for example, for the Silhouette Dog Coat. Unlike the previous hand stitches, this stitch is sewn to be seen.

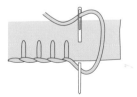

Secure a contrasting yarn to the edge of the knitting. Bring the needle up from the wrong side of the knitting, about 1/4in (6mm) in from the edge, making a diagonal stitch. When you make the next stitch, 1/4in (6mm) away from the last stitch, take the needle through the loop formed and pull down to make a right angle at the edge of the knitting.

FINISHING TECHNIQUES

Finishing your knitting is an essential moment. You can either produce a perfectly finished accessory or ruin a beautifully knitted accessory.

WEAVING IN THE LOOSE YARN ENDS

Using a large tapestry needle with a blunt point (or a yarn needle), darn the loose ends into the back of the work and cut off.

When sewing in ends on intarsia-work, weave them through the back of the same color.

PRESSING

Press all the knitted pieces before sewing seams unless your instructions state otherwise. The yarn label will give you precise pressing and care instructions for that particular yarn, but here are a few hints:

• Cover the knitting with a clean, damp cloth and press ligthly with a steam iron. Do not drag the iron over the knitting, but instead lift it gently up and down.
• Press stockinette stitch and especially intarsia-work more firmly, blocking if necessary.
• Press ribbing extremely lightly or avoid (you do not want to flatten it as it will loose its spring).
• Garter stitch needs only a very light pressing or none at all.

KNITTING REMEDIES

Occasionally, when knitting, minor disasters occur. Here are two handy knitting remedies.

PICKING UP DROPPED STITCHES

If a stitch drops off the needle, you can usually pick it up with the tip of the other needle and pop it back on. If the stitch has dropped down several rows and formed a run, however, you will need to use a crochet hook.

Working from the front of the work, insert the hook into the center of dropped stitch, pick up the next bar between two stitches and draw it through to form a new stitch. Repeat this until you reach the row you are working on.

DARNING HOLES

Darning is a very useful skill to learn, although almost impossible to perfect. Animals, perhaps, won't look after your beautifully made accessories as you would like them to, so holes may appear here or there. It is far better to repair any holes than to leave them to get bigger.

Try to find some yarn to roughly match the accessory. If it is too thick, you can untwist it and separate the strands to make it finer. Using a blunt-ended tapestry or yarn needle, loosely stitch from one side of the hole to the other—you are making a "mesh base" to weave through. The idea of darning is to replace the hole in the knitting, so do not pull the sides of the hole together.

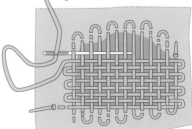

Once you have a "mesh base," weave the yarn in and out. Continue until the repair is as firm and secure as possible.

CUSTOMIZING YOUR KNITS

DESIGNING MOTIFS ON GRAPH PAPER

If you want to create a unique motif for your pet's accessory—your horse's favorite food for the blanket, your dog's favorite toy on his coat, your lucky number on the Soccer Coat, for instance—use this method:

Purchase a large sheet of graph paper from an art or stationery store. Bear in mind that there are generally more stitches than rows per inch (centimeter) so you will need to elongate your object when you draw it on the paper. (If you like, you can download graph paper tailored to your gauge at: www.thedietdiary.com.) Copy the image that you want to use onto the graph paper. Each square of the graph paper will represent one stitch, so simply color in the squares depending on what color yarn you would like to use. Now you can get on with customizing your pet's accessory.

ALPHABET

We have included an alphabet for you to use if you want to knit your pet's name, as on the Horse Blanket. You can also use it on a dog coat, cat cushion, or anywhere else you wish. See page 140.

KNITTING ABBREVIATIONS

The following are the abbreviations used in this book. Special abbreviations are given with individual patterns.

alt	alternate
beg	begin(ning)
cm	centimeter(s)
cont	continu(e)(ing)
dec	decreas(e)(ing)
DK	double knitting (a lightweight yarn)
foll	follow(s)(ing)
g	gram(s)
in	inch(es)
inc	increas(e)(ing)
k	knit
k2tog	knit next 2 sts together
m	meter(s)
MC	main color (of yarn)
mm	millimeter(s)
oz	ounce(s)
p	purl
p2tog	purl next 2 sts together
patt	pattern
psso	pass slipped stitch over
rem	remain(s)(ing)
rep	repeat(s)(ing)
rev St st	reverse stockinette stitch; purl sts on RS rows and knit sts on WS rows
RS	right side
sl	slip
st(s)	stitch(es)
St st	stockinette stitch; knit sts on RS rows and purl sts on WS rows
tbl	through back loop(s)
tog	together
WS	wrong side
yo	yarn over (yarn over right-hand needle to make a new stitch)
*	Repeat instructions after asterisk or between asterisks as many times as instructed.
[ ]	Repeat instructions inside square brackets as many times as instructed
-	Where a hyphen appears instead of a number, it means that instructions do not apply to that size

DIFFICULTY RATING (shown at beginning of each pattern)

Easy

Intermediate

Difficult

THE PROJECTS

BEANBAGS FOR **CAT** OR **DOG**

Here's a cocooning, comfortable beanbag for your pet to relax into that will look enchanting in any living room. Blend the colors to go with your pet or house. The beanbag comes in three sizes designed for cats and dogs—or any stray animal that wants to curl up.

BEANBAGS FOR **CAT** OR **DOG**

LEVEL

Knitted beanbag cover: Easy
Beanbag fabric cushion: Intermediate

SIZES

Choose your size as follows:
Small—for a cat
Medium—for a small/medium dog
Large—for a large dog

The finished beanbag measures approximately 22 (25: 28)in/ 55 (62.5: 70)cm in diameter across the circular base, and each of the four top segments (which form the top and sides of the bag) measures 17 (22: 27)in/43 (55.5: 68.5)cm from the cast-on edge to the tip at the center of the beanbag.

MATERIALS

Knitted beanbag cover
Approximately $22\frac{3}{4}$ ($26\frac{1}{4}$: $29\frac{3}{4}$)oz/650 (750: 850)g of a selection of balls of Rowan *Scottish Tweed Aran*, Rowan *Pure Wool DK*, and Jaeger *Matchmaker Merino DK* in a total of 10–13 different colors (see the Special Yarn Note on page 24)
Small amount of Jaeger *Fur* (optional)
Pair of size 9 (5.5mm) knitting needles
4 large snaps
Beanbag cushion
Newspaper, or other large sheets of paper, for paper pattern
Approximately $2\frac{1}{4}$ ($2\frac{1}{2}$: $2\frac{3}{4}$)yd/2 (2.2: 2.5)m of 45in/112cm wide calico or other cotton fabric remnant, and matching sewing thread
18in/45cm zipper
18oz/500g of polystyrene balls, for cushion filling

GAUGE

16 sts and 30 rows to 4in/10cm measured over garter stitch using size 9 (5.5mm) needles and Rowan *Scottish Tweed Aran*.

ABBREVIATIONS

See page 17.

SPECIAL YARN NOTE

Use the Rowan *Scottish Tweed Aran* yarn **single** when knitting the beanbag, but use the Rowan *Pure Wool DK* or Jaeger *Matchmaker Merino DK* **double**. Use Jaeger *Fur* sparingly, introducing it across only one or two rows in the top segments of the beanbag.

The yarns specified are only suggestions, as this project provides an ideal opportunity for you to use up leftover yarns in a variety of textures—the more textured the beanbag, the more interesting it will be. Remember to use your leftover Aran-weight yarn single, your leftover double-knitting-weight yarn double, and very thick yarns (like the Jaeger *Fur*) only in a couple of rows. Prepare the yarn as explained before beginning your knitting.

KNITTED BEANBAG COVER

TO PREPARE THE YARN

Cut the Aran-weight yarn into varying lengths—approximately 12in/30.5cm to 36in/92cm long. Cut the double-knitting-weight yarn to twice this length. Fold the double-knitting weight yarns in half so that they are double (see the Special Yarn Note, above), then knot the lengths together, end to end, introducing the colors randomly. (To reduce the number of knots, you can link the doubled yarn together at the fold where possible.)

Note: When you are knitting, try to position the knots on the wrong side of the work. If the occasional knot does pop through onto the right side, it is easy to push it back to the wrong side when you reach it on the next row.

BASE PIECES (MAKE 2)

With size 9 (5.5mm) needles and prepared yarn, cast on 88 (100: 112) sts. Mark 14th (20th: 26th) cast-on st and 74th (80th: 86th) cast-on st with a colored thread to show position of opening on base of beanbag.
Work 20 rows in garter st (knit every row). Cont in garter st throughout, dec 1 st at each end of next row and then at each end of every foll alt row 28 (30: 32) times in all. (*32 (40: 48) sts.*)
Dec 1 st at each end of next 6 (10: 14) rows.
Bind off rem 20 sts knitwise.
Make second base piece in same way.

TOP SEGMENTS (MAKE 4)

With size 9 (5.5mm) needles, cast on 74 (80: 86) sts.
Work 40 (70: 100) rows in garter st (knit every row).
Cont in garter st throughout, dec 1 st at each end of next row and then at each end of every foll 3rd row 26 (29: 32) times in all. (*22 sts.*)
Next row *K2tog, k3; rep from * to last 2 sts, k2tog. (*17 sts.*)

Work 2 rows in garter st.
Next row *K2tog, k2; rep from * to last 5 sts, k2tog, k1, k2tog. (*12 sts.*)
Work 2 rows in garter st.
Next row K2tog, k1, [k2tog] 3 times, k1, k2tog. (*7 sts.*)
Work 2 rows in garter st.
Next row K2tog, k3tog, k2tog. (*3 sts.*)
Work 1 row in garter st.
Next row K3tog, break off yarn, thread tail end through rem st, and pull tight to fasten off.

TO FINISH

Darn in all yarn ends and push all knots on right side through to wrong side.
Press all pieces lightly on wrong side, following instructions on yarn label.
Using a single strand of a double-knitting-weight yarn, sew pieces together as follows:
With right sides together, sew two base pieces together along cast-on edges, stitching from side edges to markers (leaving a large opening between markers for inserting cushion). Remove markers.
Sew together four top segments, stitching from tips (which are at center of cover) to cast-on edge.
Sew cast-on edge of top to base, aligning seams on base with two of segment seams.
Sew four large snaps, equally spaced apart, to opening.

BEANBAG CUSHION

PAPER PATTERN PIECES

Use newspaper or other large sheets of paper to make the paper pattern for the cushion. (The cushion is circular, and once inserted in the knitted cover, it gives the beanbag its circular shape.)

Pattern piece for circular base

Cut a paper rectangle 11½ (13: 14½)in/ 29 (33: 36.5)cm by 23 (26: 29)in/ 58 (66: 73)cm.

Fold the rectangle in half to make a square. Using a homemade compass and measuring from one of the corners at the fold, mark 11½ (13: 14½)in/29 (33: 36.5)cm from this corner and in a curve from the adjacent corner across the square to the opposite corner. Keeping the paper folded, cut along the marked curve, then open out the semicircle. (This finished pattern piece includes the seam allowance along the curved edge, but not along the straight edge.) Mark the position for the 18in/45cm zipper at the center of the straight edge of the semicircle.

Pattern piece for top segments

Cut a paper rectangle 18 (20½: 23)in/ 46 (52: 58)cm by 17 (22: 27)in/ 43 (55.5: 68.5)cm.

Then shape this rectangle into the shape of one of the four top segments of the cushion as follows:

Lay the rectangle with an edge 18 (20.5: 23)in/46 (52: 58)cm long at the bottom—this edge is the base of the segment. Measure up from the base 5 (7: 9)in/ 12.5 (17.5: 22.5)cm along both the right and left side edge of the rectangle and make a mark.

Find the center of the top edge of the rectangle (you can fold the rectangle in half to find the center) and mark. Then draw a gentle curve from the center of the top of the rectangle to each of the marks made at the side edges.

Cut along the curves. (This finished pattern piece does not include seam allowances.)

TO CUT FABRIC PIECES

Using the pattern for the circular base, cut two base pieces from the fabric, adding an extra ½in/1.5cm along the straight edge of the paper pattern for the seam allowance at the center of the cushion. Mark the position for the zipper on each of these pieces. Using the pattern for the top segments, cut four top segments from the fabric, adding an extra ½in/1.5cm all around the paper pattern for the seam allowance.

TO SEW THE CUSHION

Pin the two base pieces together along the straight edges, with right sides together. Taking a ½in/1.5cm seam allowance throughout, stitch the seam, leaving a 18in/45cm opening for the zipper as marked. Press the seam open and press ½in/1.5cm to the wrong side along the zipper opening. Stitch the zipper in place and set the cushion base aside.

With right sides together, pin two top segments together along one curved edge, and stitch. Stitch the two remaining top segments together in the same way. Pin the two halves of the top together and stitch, to make a large cone shape.

Open the zipper, then pin the cone-shaped top to the base, with right sides together and aligning the base seams with two of the top segments seams (ease in the top as necessary to fit the base). Stitch along this seam twice (for strength).

Clip the seam allowances around the curves as necessary, so that the seams lie flat. Press.

Turn right side out. Fill the cushion with polystyrene balls until it is about one third full and zipper the opening closed.

Insert the cushion in the knitted beanbag cover and snap closed.

CARROT CURTAIN

Why should your poor rabbit languish with almost no interior décor in its hutch? You can now show you care by giving its home a makeover with these easy-to-knit and cheery curtains. If you don't have a rabbit but have a pet guinea pig instead, you can always substitute the carrots for something that guinea pigs like—dandelion leaves, green bell peppers, cow parsley, or grass.

CARROT CURTAIN

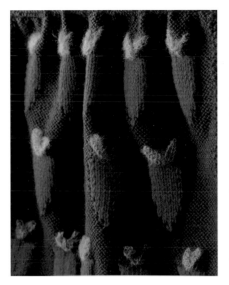

LEVEL
Intermediate

SIZE
The finished carrot curtain measures approximately 14in/35.5cm wide by 12½in/32cm long.

Note: The curtain can be made wider or longer to fit your hutch by adding more stitches or rows.

MATERIALS
2 x 1¾oz/50g balls of Rowan *Pure Wool DK* in main color **MC** (dark gray/Anthracite 003), for background
1 x 1¾oz/50g ball of Rowan *Pure Wool DK* in **A** (orange/Quarry 035), for carrots
1 x ⅞oz/25g ball of Rowan *Kidsilk Haze* in **B** (green/Jelly 597), for carrot stalks
Pair of size 6 (4mm) knitting needles
Wooden dowel, 17in/43cm long by ¼in/6mm in diameter, for curtain pole
2 metal screw-in hooks, for attaching dowel to front of hutch

GAUGE
22 sts and 30 rows to 4in/10cm measured over St st using size 6 (4mm) needles and MC.

ABBREVIATIONS
See page 17.

CHART NOTE
The background in the center of the curtain is worked in reverse stockinette stitch and the carrot motifs in stockinette stitch. There is a 5-stitch seed stitch border along each side edge of the curtain center to form firm edges.

When working from the chart, read odd-numbered rows (right-side rows) from right to left, and even-numbered rows (wrong-side rows) from left to right.

When working the carrot motifs, use the intarsia method (see page 14), knitting with a separate small ball (or long length) of yarn for each area of color and twisting yarns together on wrong side when changing color to avoid holes.

The carrot stalks are knitted separately and sewn onto the completed curtain.

TO MAKE CURTAIN
With size 6 (4mm) needles and MC, cast on 83 sts.
Work lower border in seed st as follows:
1st seed st row (RS) K1, *p1, k1; rep from * to end.
(Last row is repeated to form seed st.)
Work 9 rows more in seed st, ending with a WS row.
Set patt for center as follows:
1st patt row (RS) K1, [p1, k1] twice, p to last 5 sts, [k1, p1] twice, k1.
2nd patt row K1, [p1, k1] twice, K to last 5 sts, [k1, p1] twice, k1.
Rep last 2 rows once more, ending

with a WS row.
Using MC and A as required, position carrot motifs (see page 126) on next 2 rows (chart rows 5 and 6) as follows:
Next row (RS) Using MC k1, [p1, k1] twice, p8, *using A k1, using MC p13; rep from * 3 times more, using A k1, using MC p8, [k1, p1] twice, k1.
Next row Using MC k1, [p1, k1] twice, k8, *using A p1, using MC k13; rep from * 3 times more, using A p1, using MC k8, [k1, p1] twice, k1.
Cont as set, keeping 5-st side borders in seed st and following chart for 73 center sts (working carrot motifs in St st and A, and background in rev St st and MC) until all 78 chart rows have been completed, ending with a WS row.
Break off A.
Rep 1st and 2nd patt rows 5 times, ending with a WS row.
Next row (RS) Rep 2nd patt row (to form a p-st ridge on WS).
Rep 2nd patt row once more.
Rep 1st and 2nd patt rows 4 times more.
Bind off in patt.

CARROT STALKS (MAKE 14)
With size 6 (4mm) needles and B, cast on 15 sts.
Bind off 15 sts knitwise.
Make 13 more carrot stalks in same way.

TO FINISH
Block and press curtain lightly on wrong side, following instructions on yarn label.
Fold each stalk into a V-shape as shown, and sew one to top of each of 14 carrot motifs on curtain, using B.
Fold bound-off edge at top of curtain to wrong side and slip stitch bound-off edge to ridge row to form a channel at top of curtain. Insert curtain pole into channel.
Screw two metal hooks to hutch, and slide curtain pole in place on hooks.

DOG COATS

We have designed a range of coats to suit your dog's every whim. The Soccer Coat will give your dog a sense of purpose when playing with a ball. In an equally manly vein, there is the simple, timelessly elegant Cable Coat. One of our most practical garments, it has a masculine Sean Connery feel combined with contemporary retro chic. As we all know, spots never go out of fashion, and any dog wearing the Britart-inspired Spot Dog Coat will feel equally at home in Central Park or the backyard. Finally, ravishing yet practical, the Floral Dog Coat is for the dog who wants to stand out from the crowd. For an extravagant occasion, team it with the Floral Party Dog Collar on page 66.

SOCCER **DOG** COAT

LEVEL
Intermediate

SIZES
See page 10 for dog measurements and sizes.

FINISHED COAT MEASUREMENTS

	Width of coat	Length to neck shaping
Extra small	14in/35.5cm	12in/30.5cm
Small	15³/₄in/40cm	14in/35.5cm
Medium	18¹/₂in/47cm	18in/45.5cm
Large	24in/61cm	22in/55.5cm
Extra large	26¹/₂in/67cm	24in/61cm

MATERIALS
2 (2: 3: 4: 5) x 1³/₄oz/50g balls of Jaeger *Matchmaker Merino DK* in
main color **MC**
1 x 1³/₄oz/50g ball of Jaeger *Matchmaker Merino DK* in a contrasting color **A**
Pair of size 3 (3.25mm) knitting needles
Pair of size 6 (4mm) knitting needles
Set of four size 3 (3.25mm) double-pointed knitting needles

GAUGE
22 sts and 30 rows to 4in/10cm measured over St st using size 6
(4mm) needles.

ABBREVIATIONS
See page 17.

CHART NOTE
The charts are worked in St st. When
working from the charts, read odd-
numbered rows (k rows) from right to left,
and even-numbered rows (p rows) from
left to right.
When working the chart patterns, use the
intarsia method (see page 14), knitting
with a separate small ball (or long length)
of yarn for each area of color and twisting
yarns together on wrong side when
changing color to avoid holes.

TOP OF COAT
With size 3 (3.25mm) needles and MC,
cast on 42 (46: 56: 76: 86) sts.
1st rib row (RS) *K1, p1; rep from * to end.
(Last row is repeated to form k1, p1
rib patt.)
Work 3 rows more in rib, ending with
a WS row.
Change to A and work 2 rows more
in rib.
Break off A.
Cont with MC only, work 4 rows more
in rib.
Change to size 6 (4mm) needles.
Beg St st with rib borders as follows:
Next row (RS) [K1, p1] twice, k into front
and back of next st, k to last 5 sts, k into
front and back of next st, [k1, p1] twice.
Next row Rib 4 sts as set, p to last 4 sts,
rib 4 sts as set.
Rep last 2 rows 7 (9: 9: 11: 11) times,
ending with a WS row.
(58 (66: 76: 100: 110) sts.)

Extra Small and Small only
Cont in St st only, set position of number
chart (see page 126) as follows:
Next row (RS) K27 (31: -: -: -)MC, k5A,
k26 (30: -: -: -)MC.
Next row P24 (28: -: -: -)MC, p10A,
p24 (28: -: -: -)MC.

Medium, Large, and Extra Large only

Work even as set, with St st at center and 4-st rib border along each side edge, until work measures - (-: 5½: 7: 8)in/ - (-: 14: 17.5: 20)cm from cast-on edge (measuring up center of panel), ending with a WS row.
Set position of number chart (see page 126) as follows:
Next row (RS) Rib 4 sts in MC, k- (-: 32: 44: 49)MC, k5A, k- (-: 31: 43: 48)MC, rib 4 sts in MC.
Next row Rib 4 sts in MC, p- (-: 29: 41: 46)MC, p10A, p- (-: 29: 41: 46)MC, rib 4 sts in MC.
Cont foll chart as set and working 4-st rib borders until work measures - (-: 6: 8: 9)in/ - (-: 15: 20: 22.5)cm from cast-on edge, ending with a WS row.

All sizes

Beg with a k row, work all sts in St st and cont foll chart until all 40 chart rows have been completed (then cont with MC only) **and at the same time** cont in patt as now set until work measures 5½ (7 :11: 13: 14)in/14 (17.5: 28: 33: 35.5)cm from cast-on edge, ending with a p row.
(**Note:** If required, increase or reduce length of coat here and match this change on gusset.)

Mark for leg openings

Mark each end of last row with a colored thread to indicate beg of leg openings.
Cont in St st until work measures 8 (10: 14: 16 : 17½)in/20 (25.5: 35.5: 40.5: 44.5)cm from cast-on edge, ending with a p row.
Mark each end of last row with a colored thread to indicate end of leg openings.
Cont in St st until work measures 10 (12: 16: 18: 20)in/25.5 (30.5: 40.5: 45.5: 50.5)cm, ending with a p row.
Next row (RS) K8 (10: 12: 18: 20), k2tog, k to last 10 (12: 14: 20: 22) sts, k2tog, k8 (10: 12: 18: 20).
Purl 1 row.
Rep last 2 rows row 5 (7: 8: 14: 14) times. (46 (50: 58: 70: 80) sts.)
Work even in St st until work measures 12 (14: 18: 22: 24)in/30.5 (35.5: 45.5: 55.5: 61)cm from cast-on edge, ending with a p row.
Break off yarn and leave sts on a st holder.

GUSSET

With size 3 (3.25mm) needles and MC, cast on 16 (22: 28: 34: 38) sts.
Work 4 rows in k1, p1 rib as for top of coat.
Change to A and work 2 rows more in rib.
Break off A.
Cont with MC only, work 2 rows more in rib.
Change to size 6 (4mm) needles.
Beg with a k row, work in St st until gusset measures 3½ (3: 5: 5: 5)in/6.5 (7.5: 13: 13: 13)cm from cast-on edge, ending with a p row.

Mark for leg openings

Mark each end of last row with a colored thread to indicate beg of leg openings.
Cont in St st throughout, work until leg openings measure same as leg openings on top of coat, ending with a p row.
Mark each end of last row with a colored thread to indicate end of leg openings.
Work until gusset measures 6 (7: 9: 10: 12)in/15 (17.5: 22.5: 25: 30.5)cm from cast-on edge, ending with a p row.
Set position of badge chart (see page 126) as follows:
Next row (RS) K7 (10: 13: 16: 18)MC, k1A, k8 (11: 14: 17: 19)MC.
Next row P7 (10: 13: 16: 18)MC, p3A, p6 (9: 12: 15: 17)MC.
Cont in St st foll chart as set until chart row 20 has been completed (then cont with MC only) **and at the same time** cont as set until work measures 8 (8½: 10½: 10: 12)in/20 (21.5: 26.5: 25: 30.5)cm from cast-on edge, ending with a p row.
Dec 1 st at each end of next 4 (6: 9: 11: 12) rows, ending with a p (p: k: k: p) row. (8 (10: 10: 12: 14) sts.)
Work even until gusset measures 9 (10: 12: 14: 15)in/23 (25.5: 30.5: 35.5: 38.5)cm from cast-on edge, ending with a p row.
Break off yarn and leave first 4 (5: 5: 6: 7) sts on one st holder and rem 4 (5: 5: 6: 7) sts on another st holder.

TO FINISH

Press top of coat and gusset lightly on wrong side, following instructions on yarn label and avoiding ribbing.

With right sides together and matching leg-opening markers, sew gusset to top of coat, leaving seam open between markers for front-leg openings.
Turn coat right side out.

Collar

The collar is worked so that it is divided at the center front (under the chin) after 4 rows in rib.
With RS facing and using set of four size 3 (3.25mm) double-pointed needles and A, k 4 (5: 5: 6: 7) sts from left gusset st holder, k 46 (50: 58: 70: 80) sts from top-of-coat st holder and k 4 (5: 5: 6: 7) sts from right gusset st holder (distributing sts evenly on 3 needles and knitting with 4th needle). (54 (60: 68: 82: 94) sts.)
Work 4 rounds in k1, p1 rib, ending at center front.
Now turn work and start working collar back and forth in rows of garter st (knit every row) so that it is divided at center front as follows:
Next row (RS of collar) K13 (15: 17: 20: 23), k into front and back of next st, k to last 14 (16: 18: 21: 24) sts, k into front and back of next st, k13 (15: 17: 20: 23).
Next row (WS of collar) K to end.
Rep last 2 rows 7 times, ending with a WS row.
Change to MC and knit 2 rows.
Break off MC.
Change to A and knit 4 rows.
Bind off knitwise.

Edging on front leg openings

With RS facing and using set of four size 3 (3.25mm) double-pointed needles and A, pick up and knit 30 (38: 38: 46: 46) sts around one front leg opening.
Work 6 rounds in k1, p1 rib.
Change to MC and work 1 round more in rib.
Break off MC.
Change to A and work 2 rounds more in rib.
Bind off loosely in rib.
Work second edging in same way.

C A B L E **D O G** C O A T

LEVEL
Easy

SIZES
See page 10 for dog measurements and sizes.

FINISHED COAT MEASUREMENTS

	Width of coat	Length to neck shaping
Extra small	12$\frac{1}{4}$in/31cm	12in/30.5cm
Small	14$\frac{3}{4}$in/37.5cm	14in/35.5cm
Medium	17$\frac{3}{4}$in/45cm	18in/45.5cm
Large	23in/58.5cm	22in/55.5cm
Extra large	25$\frac{1}{2}$in/65cm	24in/61cm

MATERIALS
2 (2: 2: 3: 4) x 1$\frac{3}{4}$oz/50g balls of Rowan *Felted Tweed*
Pair of size 3 (3.25mm) knitting needles
Pair of size 6 (4mm) knitting needles
Short double-pointed size 6 (4mm) knitting needle or cable needle

GAUGE
22 sts and 30 rows to 4in/10cm measured over St st using size 6 (4mm) needles.
14-stitch cable panel measures approximately 1$\frac{1}{2}$in/4cm wide.

ABBREVIATIONS
C10B = slip next 5 sts onto cable needle and hold at back of work, k5, then k5 from cable needle.
Also see page 17

TOP OF COAT
With size 3 (3.25mm) needles, cast on 42 (46: 56: 76: 86) sts.
1st rib row *K1, p1; rep from * to end.
(Last row is repeated to form k1, p1 rib patt.)
Work 5 rows more in rib.
Change to size 6 (4mm) needles.
Beg cable patt as follows:
1st patt row (RS) [K1, p1] twice, k into front and back of next st, k9 (11: 16: 26: 31); for cable panel, work p2, k10, p2; k9 (11: 16: 26: 31), k into front and back of next st, [k1, p1] twice.
(44 (48: 58: 78: 88) sts.)

2nd patt row [K1, p1] twice, p11 (13: 18: 28: 33); for cable panel, work k2, p10, k2; p11 (13: 18: 28: 33), [k1, p1] twice.
3rd patt row [K1, p1] twice, k into front and back of next st, k10 (12: 17: 27: 32); for cable panel, work p2, k10, p2; k10 (12: 17: 27: 32), k into front and back of next st, [k1, p1] twice.
(46 (50: 60: 80: 90) sts.)
4th patt row [K1, p1] twice, p12 (14: 19: 29: 34); for cable panel, work k2, p10, k2; p12 (14: 19: 29: 34), [k1, p1] twice.
5th patt row [K1, p1] twice, k into front and back of next st, k11 (13: 18: 28:

33); for cable panel, work p2, k10, p2; k11 (13: 18: 28: 33), k into front and back of next st, [k1, p1] twice.
(48 (52: 62: 82: 92) sts.)
6th patt row [K1, p1] twice, p13 (15: 20: 30: 35); for cable panel, work k2, p10, k2; p13 (15: 20: 30: 35), [k1, p1] twice.
7th patt row [K1, p1] twice, k into front and back of next st, k12 (14: 19: 29: 34); for cable panel, work p2, C10B, p2; k12 (14: 19: 29: 34), k into front and back of next st, [k1, p1] twice.
(50 (54: 64: 84: 94) sts.)
This sets patt with St st at each side of a

35

central 14-st cable panel and a 4-st rib border along each side edge.

Cont in patt as set, crossing cable (as in 7th patt row) on every foll 10th row, **and at the same time** cont to inc 1 st at each end (inside rib borders) of 4 (6: 6: 8: 8) foll alt rows (RS rows), ending with a RS row. (58 (66: 76: 100: 110) sts.)

Work even in patt as set until cable panel measures 3 (4: 6: 8: 9)in/7.5 (10: 15: 20: 22.5)cm from cast-on edge, ending with a WS row.

Next row (RS) K22 (26: 31: 43: 48); work next 14 sts in cable panel patt as set; k22 (26: 31: 43: 48).

Next row P22 (26: 31: 43: 48); work next 14 sts in cable panel patt as set; p22 (26: 31: 43: 48).

This sets patt with St st at each side of central 14-st cable panel.

Cont in patt as now set until cable panel measures 5½ (7: 11: 13: 14)in/ 14 (17.5: 28: 33: 35.5)cm from cast-on edge, ending with a WS row.

(**Note:** If required, increase or reduce length of coat here and match this change on gusset.)

Mark for leg openings

Mark each end of last row with a colored thread to indicate beg of leg openings.
Cont in patt until cable panel measures 8 (10: 14: 16: 17½)in/20 (25.5: 35.5: 40.5: 44.5)cm from cast-on edge, ending with a WS row.

Mark each end of last row with a colored thread to indicate end of leg openings.
Cont in patt until cable panel measures 10 (12: 16: 18: 20)in/25.5 (30.5: 40.5: 45.5: 50.5)cm from cast-on edge, ending with a WS row.

Next row (RS) K8 (10: 12: 18: 20), k2tog, k12 (14: 17: 23: 26); work next 14 sts in cable panel patt as set; k12 (14: 17: 23: 26), k2tog, k8 (10: 12: 18: 20). (56 (64: 74: 98: 108) sts.)

Next row P21 (25: 30: 42: 47); work next 14 sts in cable panel patt as set; p21 (25: 30: 42: 47).

Next row K8 (10: 12: 18: 20), k2tog, k11 (13: 16: 22: 25); work next 14 sts in cable panel patt as set; k11 (13: 16: 22: 25), k2tog, k8 (10: 12: 18: 20). (54 (62: 72: 96: 106) sts.)

Working in patt as set, cont to dec 1 st at each end of 4 (6: 7: 13: 13) foll alt rows (RS rows), ending with a RS row. (46 (50: 58: 70: 80) sts.)

Work even in patt until cable panel measures 12 (14: 18: 22: 24)in/ 30.5 (35.5: 45.5: 55.5: 61)cm from cast-on edge, ending with a WS row.
Break off yarn and leave sts on a st holder.

GUSSET

With size 3 (3.25mm) needles, cast on 16 (22: 28: 34: 38) sts.
Work 6 rows in k1, p1 rib as for top of coat.
Change to size 6 (4mm) needles.
Beg with a k row, work in St st until gusset measures 3½ (3: 5: 5: 5)in/6.5 (7.5: 13: 13: 13)cm from cast-on edge, ending with a p row.

Mark for leg openings

Mark each end of last row with a colored thread to indicate beg of leg openings.
Cont in St st throughout, work until leg openings measure same as leg openings on top of coat, ending with a p row.
Mark each end of last row with a colored

thread to indicate end of leg openings.
Work until gusset measures 8 (8½: 10½: 10: 12)in/20 (21.5: 26.5: 25.5: 30.5)cm from cast-on edge, ending with a p row.

Dec 1 st at each end of next 4 (6: 9: 11: 12) rows, ending with a p (p: k: k: p) row. (8 (10: 10: 12: 14) sts.)

Work even until gusset measures 9 (10: 12: 14: 15)in/23 (25.5: 30.5: 35.5: 38.5)cm from cast-on edge, ending with a p row.
Do not break off yarn and leave sts on a st holder.

TO FINISH

Press top of coat and gusset lightly on wrong side, following instructions on yarn label and avoiding cable panel.
With right sides together and matching leg-opening markers, sew right side edge of top of coat to left side edge of gusset, leaving seam open between markers for front-leg openings.

Turtleneck collar

With RS facing and size 3 (3.25mm) needles, k 8 (10: 10: 12: 14) sts from gusset st holder and k 46 (50: 58: 70: 80) sts from top-of-coat st holder. (54 (60: 68: 82: 94) sts.)

Work these sts in k1, p1 rib until collar measures 4 (4: 5: 6: 6)in/10 (10: 12.5: 15: 15)cm.
Bind off loosely in rib.
With right sides together, sew remaining side seam as for first side seam, and sew collar seam reversing seam on last 2 (2: 2½: 3: 3)in/5 (5: 6.5: 7.5: 7.5)cm of collar for turnback.

SPOT **DOG** COAT

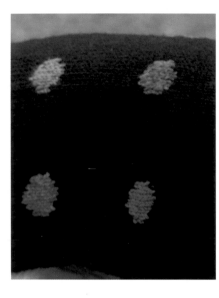

LEVEL
Intermediate

SIZES
See page 10 for dog measurements and sizes.

FINISHED COAT MEASUREMENTS

	Width of coat	Length to neck shaping
Extra small	10in/25cm	10in/25cm
Small	14in/35.5cm	13in/33cm
Medium	15$\frac{1}{2}$in/39cm	16in/40.5cm
Large	17in/43cm	20in/50.5cm
Extra large	19$\frac{3}{4}$in/50cm	22in/56cm

MATERIALS
2 (2: 2: 3: 4) x 1$\frac{3}{4}$oz/50g balls of Jaeger *Matchmaker Merino DK* in main color **MC**, for background
Small amount of Jaeger *Matchmaker Merino DK* in each of 6 different colors, for spot motifs
Pair of size 3 (3.25mm) knitting needles
Pair of size 6 (4mm) knitting needles
4 (5: 5: 5: 5) buttons

GAUGE
22 sts and 30 rows to 4in/10cm measured over St st using size 6 (4mm) needles.

ABBREVIATIONS
See page 17.

CHART NOTE
The chart is worked in St st. When working from the chart, read odd-numbered rows (k rows) from right to left, and even-numbered rows (p rows) from left to right.
When working the chart pattern, use the intarsia method (see page 14), knitting with a separate small ball (or long length) of yarn for each area of color and twisting yarns together on wrong side when changing color to avoid holes.
Note: The chart shows only the St st section of the coat; the seed stitch borders are not included on the chart.

TO MAKE COAT
With size 3 (3.25mm) needles and MC, cast on 42 (64: 72: 80: 96) sts.
Work border in seed st as follows:
1st row (RS) *K1, p1; rep from * to end.
2nd row P1, k1; rep from * to end.
3rd row [K1, p1] twice, k into front and back of next st, *p1, k1; rep from * to last 7 sts, p1, k into front and back of next st, [p1, k1] twice, p1.
(44 (66: 74: 82: 98) sts.)
4th row [P1, k1] 3 times, k next st (inc st), p1, k1; rep from * to last 7 sts, p1, k next st (inc st), [k1, p1] twice, k1.
5th row [K1, p1] twice, k into front and

back of next st, *k1, p1; rep from * to last 7 sts, k into front and back of next st, [k1, p1] 3 times.
(46 (68: 76: 84: 100) sts.)
6th row Rep 2nd row.
Change to size 6 (4mm) needles.
Cont to shape coat, beg St st patt with seed st side borders as follows:
1st patt row (RS) K1, [p1, k1] twice for seed st border; k into front and back of next st, k to last 6 sts, k into front and back of next st; p1, [k1, p1] twice for seed st border.
2nd patt row P1, [k1, p1] twice for seed st border; p to last 5 sts; k1,

[p1, k1] twice for seed st border.
3rd and 4th patt rows Rep 1st and 2nd
patt rows. (50 (72: 80: 88: 104) sts.)
Set position of chart patt (see page 127)
on next 2 rows (chart rows 5 and 6)
as follows:
5th patt row (RS) Using MC seed st 5 sts;
using MC k into front and back of next st,
k0 (2: 6: 1: 0)MC, [k2 in chosen spot
color, k16MC] 2 (3: 3: 4: 5) times, k2
in chosen spot color, k0 (2: 6: 1: 0)MC,
using MC k into front and back of next st;
using MC seed st 5 sts.
(52 (74: 82: 90: 106) sts.)
6th patt row Using MC seed st 5 sts;
p1 (3: 7: 2: 1)MC, [p4 in random spot
color, p14MC] 2 (3: 3: 4: 5) times, p4 in
random spot color, using MC p to last
5 sts; seed st 5 sts.
Cont foll chart as set and working 5-st
seed st borders **and at the same time** cont
to inc 1 st at each end (inside seed st
borders) of 2 foll alt rows (RS rows),
ending with a RS row.
(56 (78: 86: 94: 110) sts.)
Work even in patt as set, using colors at
random for spots, until chart row 36 has
been completed, ending with a WS row.
Work even in patt, repeating chart rows
13–36 for spot patt, until coat measures
10 (13: 16: 20: 22)in/25 (33: 40.5:
50.5: 56)cm from cast-on edge, ending
with a WS row in MC only.
(**Note:** If you need to lengthen coat to fit
your dog, work some extra rows here
before starting neck shaping.)

Shape neck
Next row (RS) Work 23 (34: 36: 38: 44)
sts in patt, then turn, leaving rem sts on a
st holder.
Working on these sts only, cont as follows:
**Keeping patt correct throughout, dec
1 st at neck edge of next 3 rows.
Dec 1 st at neck edge of 4 (4: 4: 2: 4)
foll alt rows.
Dec 1 st at neck edge of every 4th row
1 (1: 1: 2: 1) times.
(15 (26: 28: 31: 36) sts.)
Work even until coat measures 13 (17:
21: 26: 29)in/33 (43: 53: 66: 73.5)cm
from cast-on edge, ending with a WS row.
Change to size 3 (3.25mm) needles and
MC only.**
Work 2 rows in seed st, ending with a
WS row.

Small, Medium, Large, and Extra Large only
Next row (buttonhole row) (RS) Seed st
- (3: 5: 8: 13) sts, [work 2tog, yo, seed st
7 sts] twice, work 2tog, yo, seed st 3 sts.

Extra Small only
Next row (buttonhole row) (RS) Seed st
1 st, work 2tog, yo, seed st 7 sts,
work 2tog, yo, seed st 3 sts.

All sizes
Work 3 rows in seed st.
Bind off.
With RS facing, return to rem sts, slip center
10 (10: 14: 18: 22) sts onto a st holder,
rejoin yarn and work in patt to end.
Work as for first side of neck from ** to **.
Work 6 rows in seed st.
Bind off.

STRAP
With size 3 (3.25mm) needles and MC,
cast on 13 sts.
1st row *K1, p1, rep from * to last st, k1.
(Last row is repeated to form seed st.)
Work in seed st until strap measures
2 (4½: 6: 9½: 11)in/5 (11: 15: 24:
28)cm from cast-on edge.
Next row (buttonhole row) Seed st 5 sts,
work 2tog, yo, seed st 6 sts.
Work in seed st until strap measures
3 (5½: 7: 10½: 12)in/7.5 (14: 17.5:
26.5: 30.5)cm from cast-on edge.
Rep buttonhole row.
Work in seed st until strap measures
4 (6½: 8: 1½: 13)in/10 (16.5: 20.5:
29: 33)cm from cast-on edge.

Rep buttonhole row.
Work in seed st until strap measures
5 (7½: 9: 12: 14)in/12.5 (19: 22.5:
30.5: 35.5)cm from cast-on edge.
Bind off.

TO FINISH
Block and press coat lightly on wrong
side, following instructions on yarn label
and avoiding seed st borders. Do not
press strap.

Neck edging
With RS facing, size 3 (3.25mm) needles
and MC, pick up and knit 22 (28: 32:
36: 40) sts along right neck edge (picking
up first 5 sts along edge of seed st border),
knit 10 (10: 14: 18: 22) sts from center
neck st holder, pick up and knit 22 (28:
32: 36: 40) sts up left neck edge.
(54 (66: 78: 90: 102) sts.)
Work 2 rows in seed st, ending with a
RS row.
Next row (buttonhole row) (WS) Seed st
to last 4 sts, yo, work 2tog, seed st 2 sts
(buttonhole should be in line with other
buttonholes).
Work 2 rows more in seed st. Bind off.
Sew 3 (4: 4: 4: 4) buttons to front
opening border to correspond with
buttonholes.
Sew strap to right side-edge of coat
5½ (8: 10½: 13: 15)in/14 (20.5:
26.5: 33.5: 38)cm from cast-on edge.
Sew button for strap to wrong side of left
side-edge of coat to correspond with
position of strap.

FLORAL **DOG** COAT

LEVEL
Difficult

SIZES
See page 10 for dog measurements and sizes.

FINISHED COAT MEASUREMENTS

	Width of coat	Length to neck shaping
Extra small	10in/25.5cm	10in/25cm
Small	14in/35.5cm	13in/33cm
Medium	15$\frac{1}{2}$in/39cm	16in/40.5cm
Large	17in/43cm	20in/50.5cm
Extra large	19$\frac{3}{4}$in/50cm	22in/56cm

MATERIALS
2 (2: 2: 3: 4) x 1$\frac{3}{4}$oz/50g balls of Jaeger *Matchmaker Merino DK* in main color **MC**, for background
1 x 1$\frac{3}{4}$oz/50g ball of Jaeger *Matchmaker Merino DK* in each of 4 different colors—**A**, **B**, **C**, and **D**—for motifs
Pair of size 3 (3.25mm) knitting needles
Pair of size 6 (4mm) knitting needles
4 (5: 5: 5: 5) buttons

GAUGE
22 sts and 30 rows to 4in/10cm measured over St st using size 6 (4mm) needles.

ABBREVIATIONS
See page 17.

CHART NOTE
The chart is worked in St st. When working from the chart, read odd numbered rows (k rows) from right to left, and even-numbered rows (p rows) from left to right.
When working the chart pattern, use the intarsia method (see page 14), knitting with a separate small ball (or long length) of yarn for each area of color and twisting yarns together on wrong side when changing color to avoid holes.
Note: The chart shows only the St st section of the coat; the seed stitch borders are not included on the chart.

TO MAKE COAT
With size 3 (3.25mm) needles and MC, cast on 42 (64: 72: 80: 96) sts.
Work border in seed st as follows:
1st row (RS) *K1, p1; rep from * to end.
2nd row P1, k1; rep from * to end.
3rd row [K1, p1] twice, k into front and back of next st, *p1, k1; rep from * to last 7 sts, p1, k into front and back of next st, [p1, k1] twice, p1.
(44 (66: 74: 82: 98) sts.)
4th row [P1, k1] 3 times, k next st (the inc st), p1, k1; rep from * to last 7 sts, p1, k next st (the inc st), [k1, p1] twice, k1.

5th row [K1, p1] twice, k into front and back of next st, *k1, p1; rep from * to last 7 sts, k into front and back of next st, [k1, p1] 3 times.
(46 (68: 76: 84: 100) sts.)
6th row Rep 2nd row.
Change to size 6 (4mm) needles.
Cont to shape coat, beg St st patt with seed st side borders as follows:
1st patt row (RS) K1, [p1, k1] twice for seed st border; k into front and back of next st, k to last 6 sts, k into front and back of next st; p1, [k1, p1] twice for seed st border.

2nd patt row P1, [k1, p1] twice for seed st border; p to last 5 sts; k1, [p1, k1] twice for seed st border.

3rd and 4th patt rows Rep 1st and 2nd patt rows. *(50 (72: 80: 88: 104) sts.)*

Set position of chart patt (see pages 128–129) on next 2 rows (chart rows 5 and 6) as follows:

5th patt row (RS) Using MC seed st 5 sts; using MC k into front and back of next st, k27 (38: 42: 46: 54)MC, k4A, k7 (18: 22: 26: 34)MC, using MC k into front and back of next st; using MC seed st 5 sts. *(52 (74: 82: 90: 106) sts.)*

6th patt row Using MC seed st 5 sts; p3 (14: 18: 22: 30)MC, p3A, p2MC, p6A, using MC p to last 5 sts; seed st 5 sts. Cont foll chart as set and working 5-st seed st borders **and at the same time** cont to inc 1 st at each end (inside seed st borders) of 2 foll alt rows (RS rows), ending with a RS row.

(56 (78: 86: 94: 110) sts.)

Work even in patt as set (when chart patt has been completed, cont using MC only) until coat measures 10 (13: 16: 20: 22)in/25 (33: 40.5: 50.5: 56)cm from cast-on edge, ending with a WS row.

(Note: If you need to lengthen coat to fit your dog, work some extra rows here before starting neck shaping.)

Shape neck

Next row (RS) Work 23 (34: 36: 38: 44) sts in patt, then turn, leaving rem sts on a st holder.

Working on these sts only, cont as follows:
**Keeping patt correct throughout, dec 1 st at neck edge of next 3 rows.
Dec 1 st at neck edge of 4 (4: 4: 2: 4) foll alt rows.
Dec 1 st at neck edge of every 4th row 1 (1: 1: 2: 1) times.

(15 (26: 28: 31: 36) sts.)

Work even until coat measures 13 (17: 21: 26: 29)in/33 (43: 53: 66: 73.5)cm from cast-on edge, ending with a WS row. Change to size 3 (3.25mm) needles and MC only.**

Work 2 rows in seed st, ending with a WS row.

Small, Medium, Large, and Extra Large only

Next row (buttonhole row) (RS) Seed st - (3: 5: 8: 13) sts, [work 2tog, yo, seed st 7 sts] twice, work 2tog, yo, seed st 3 sts.

Extra Small only

Next row (buttonhole row) (RS) Seed st 1 st, work 2tog, yo, seed st 7 sts, work 2tog, yo, seed st 3 sts.

All sizes

Work 3 rows in seed st.
Bind off.
With RS facing, return to rem sts, slip center 10 (10: 14: 18: 22) sts onto a st holder, rejoin yarn and work in patt to end.
Work as for first side of neck from **
to **.
Work 6 rows in seed st.
Bind off.

STRAP

With size 3 (3.25mm) needles and MC, cast on 13 sts.

1st row *K1, p1; rep from * to last st, k1. (Last row is repeated to form seed st.)

Work in seed st until strap measures 2 (4½: 6: 9½: 11)in/5 (11: 15: 24: 28)cm from cast-on edge.

Next row (buttonhole row) Seed st 5 sts, work 2tog, yo, seed st 6 sts.

Work in seed st until strap measures 3 (5½: 7: 10½: 12)in/7.5 (14: 17.5:

26.5: 30.5)cm from cast-on edge.
Rep buttonhole row.
Work in seed st until strap measures 4 (6½: 8: 11½: 13)in/10 (16.5: 20.5: 29: 33)cm from cast-on edge.
Rep buttonhole row.
Work in seed st until strap measures 5 (7½: 9: 12: 14)in/12.5 (19: 22.5: 30.5: 35.5)cm from cast-on edge.
Bind off.

TO FINISH

Block and press coat lightly on wrong side, following instructions on yarn label and avoiding seed st borders. Do not press strap.

Neck edging

With RS facing, size 3 (3.25mm) needles and MC, pick up and knit 22 (28: 32: 36: 40) sts along right neck edge (picking up first 5 sts along edge of seed st border), knit 10 (10: 14: 18: 22) sts from center neck st holder, pick up and knit 22 (28: 32: 36: 40) sts up left neck edge. *(54 (66: 78: 90: 102) sts.)*

Work 2 rows in seed st, ending with a RS row.

Next row (buttonhole row) (WS) Seed st to last 4 sts, yo, work 2tog, seed st 2 sts (buttonhole should be in line with other buttonholes).

Work 2 rows more in seed st.
Bind off.

Sew 3 (4: 4: 4: 4) buttons to front opening border to correspond with buttonholes.

Sew strap to right side-edge of coat 5½ (8: 10½: 13: 15)in/14 (20.5: 26.5: 33:5: 38)cm from cast-on edge.

Sew button for strap to wrong side of left side-edge of coat to correspond with position of strap.

CAT CUSHIONS

Here are three designs for you to make for your
beloved cat. The plain one is extremely simple,
but has tassels on the corners for your cat to toy with
during those moments of ennui; the baroque is
grander in style; and the heraldic is appropriately
aristocratic for the most princely of pets.

TASSELS **CAT** CUSHION

LEVEL
Easy ◄◄◄◄◄◄◄◄◄

SIZE
The finished cushion measures approximately 18in/46cm square.

MATERIALS
3 x 3½oz/100g balls of Rowan *Scottish Tweed Chunky* in main color **MC**, for cushion
Small amount of a double-knitting-weight yarn in a contrasting color **A**, for tassels
Pair of size 11 (8mm) knitting needles
Pillow form to fit

GAUGE
12 sts and 16 rows to 4in/10cm measured over St st using size 11 (8mm) needles.

ABBREVIATIONS
See page 17.

TO MAKE CUSHION COVER
With size 11 (8mm) needles and MC, cast on 54 sts.
Beg with a k row, work in St st until cushion measures 36in/92cm from cast-on edge, ending with a p row. Bind off.

TO FINISH
Press lightly on wrong side, following instructions on yarn label.
Sew cast-on edge of knitting to bound-off edge.

With cover right-side out, position seam just worked in center back of cushion; then sew one side seam using mattress stitch. Insert pillow form and sew other side seam in same way.

Tassels (make 4)
Cut a piece of cardboard 2in/5cm wide by 4in/10cm long.
Wind A around length of cardboard 25 times. Then thread a needle with a length of A and pass it under wrapped yarn at one end of cardboard. Tie yarn tightly,

leaving two long tail ends. Cut through strands of yarn at other end of cardboard. Wind one long tail end of yarn tightly around tassel approximately ³/₄in/2cm from uncut end and secure.
Use remaining length of yarn to sew tassel to one corner of cushion.
Make three more tassels in same way and sew one to each of the three remaining corners.

BAROQUE **CAT** CUSHION

LEVEL
Intermediate

SIZE
The finished cushion measures approximately 18in/45.5cm square.

MATERIALS
3 x 1¾oz/50g balls of Rowan *Pure Wool DK* in main color **MC**
1 x 1¾oz/50g ball of Rowan *Pure Wool DK* in a contrasting color **A**
Pair of size 6 (4mm) knitting needles
Pillow form to fit

GAUGE
22 sts and 30 rows to 4in/10cm over St st using size 6 (4mm) needles.

ABBREVIATIONS
See page 17.

CHART NOTE
The chart is worked in St st. When working from the chart, read odd-numbered rows (k rows) from right to left, and even-numbered rows (p rows) from left to right. When working the chart pattern, use the intarsia method (see page 14), knitting with a separate small ball (or long length) of yarn for each area of color and twisting yarns together on wrong side when changing color to avoid holes.

CUSHION COVER FRONT
With size 6 (4mm) needles and MC, cast on 100 sts.
Beg with a k row, work 4 rows in St st, ending with a p row.
Set position of chart patt (see page 130) on next 2 rows (chart rows 5 and 6) as follows:
Next row (RS) Using MC k35, using A k8, using MC k14, using A k8, using MC k35.
Next row Using MC p34, using A p11, using MC k10, using A p11, using MC p34.
Cont in St st following chart until chart row 132 has been completed, ending with a p row.
Using MC only and beg with a k row, work 4 rows in St st.
Bind off.

CUSHION COVER BACK
With size 6 (4mm) needles and MC, cast on 100 sts.
Beg with a k row, work 136 rows in St st.
Bind off.

TO FINISH
Block and press both pieces lightly on wrong side, following instructions on yarn label.
With right sides together, sew front to back leaving one side open.
Turn cover right side out.
Insert pillow form and sew remaining seam.

HERALDIC **CAT** CUSHION

LEVEL
Intermediate ◀‹‹‹‹‹‹◀ ◀ ◀‹‹‹‹‹‹◀

SIZE
The finished cushion measures approximately 18in/45.5cm square.

MATERIALS
2 x 1³/₄oz/50g balls of Jaeger *Matchmaker Merino DK* in main color **MC** (black/Black 681), for background
1 x 1³/₄oz/50g ball of Jaeger *Matchmaker Merino DK* in each of **A** (violet/Geranium 894), **B** (ocher/Syrup 789), and **C** (teal/Teal 790), for motifs
Pair of size 6 (4mm) knitting needles
Pillow form to fit

GAUGE
22 sts and 30 rows to 4in/10cm measured over St st using size 6 (4mm) needles.

ABBREVIATIONS
See page 17.

YARN NOTE
The colors listed in the Materials list are there merely as a suggestion. Feel free to pick your own selection of four different colors to customize the cushion. You can use Jaeger *Matchmaker Merino DK*, Rowan *Pure Wool DK*, or any other yarn of the same weight.

CHART NOTE
The chart is worked in St st. When working from the chart, read odd-numbered rows (k rows) from right to left, and even-numbered rows (p rows) from left to right. When working the chart pattern, use the intarsia method (see page 14), knitting with a separate small ball (or long length) of yarn for each area of color and twisting

yarns together on wrong side when changing color to avoid holes.

CUSHION COVER FRONT
With size 6 (4mm) needles and MC, cast on 100 sts.
Beg with a k row, work 4 rows in St st, ending with a p row.
Set position of chart patt (see page 131) on next 2 rows (chart rows 5 and 6) as follows:
Next row (RS) Using MC k46, using A k8, using MC k46.
Next row Using MC p44, using A p12, using MC p44.
Cont in St st following chart until chart row 132 has been completed, ending with a p row.

Using MC only and beg with a k row, work 4 rows in St st.
Bind off.

CUSHION COVER BACK
With size 6 (4mm) needles and MC, cast on 100 sts.
Beg with a k row, work 136 rows in St st.
Bind off.

TO FINISH
Block and press both pieces lightly on wrong side, following instructions on yarn label.
With right sides together, sew front to back leaving one side open.
Turn cover right side out.
Insert pillow form and sew remaining seam.

WATER LILY

Don't neglect your goldfish. Here is your chance to knit this beautiful water lily for nothing. In an evening, using recycled plastic bags, you can decorate your fish tank. Try making several lilies and float them in your pond outside. So much easier to look after than the real thing.

WATER LILY

LEVEL
Easy

SIZE
The finished water lily measures approximately 4–4³/₄in/10–12cm in diameter and each leaf measures approximately 3¹/₂–4in/9–10cm in length.

MATERIALS
One green plastic bag, to make "yarn" **A** for leaves
One white or pink plastic bag, to make "yarn" **B** for petals
One orange plastic bag, to make "yarn" **C** for stamens
Pair of size 6 (4mm) knitting needles
Matching sewing thread, for sewing together petals and sewing on stamens

GAUGE
It is not necessary to knit to a specific gauge to make the water lily. The size will vary (see Size above) according to the thickness of the plastic used for the "yarn," the width of the plastic strips, and the knitter's individual tension.

ABBREVIATIONS
See page 17.

SPECIAL NOTE
The plastic "yarn" is knitted in garter stitch (knit every row) in the usual way. The "yarn" will stretch while you are knitting with it, so be careful not to pull it too tightly because this might break it, and the more breaks the more knots and the more tails ends you will have to darn in later.

TO PREPARE PLASTIC "YARN"
Using scissors, cut off the bottom and handles of each bag (including gusset), so that it forms a large tube.
Cut each bag into a continuous "yarn" strip as follows:
Open out bag. Then starting at the bottom of bag, cut a continuous strip of plastic in a spiral (as you would peel an apple), about ³/₈in/1cm wide. If the bag has printing on it, you can either cut out that section or incorporate into your knitting "yarn." Loosely wind the strip into a ball as you proceed.

If the plastic breaks while you are preparing it, just knot the strips together.

LEAVES (MAKE 2)
With size 6 (4mm) needles and A, cast on 4 sts.
Knit 1 row.
Cont in garter st throughout, inc 1 st at each end of next row 5 rows. (*14 sts.*)
Knit 1 row.
Inc 1 st at each end of next row. (*16 sts.*)
Work even in garter st for 10 rows.

Divide leaf
Before beg next row to divide leaf, mark this side of work as RS, using a colored thread.
Next row (RS) K8, then turn, leaving rem sts on a st holder.
Working on these 8 sts only, cont as follows:
Knit 1 row.
Dec 1 st at beg of next row (outer leaf edge). (*7 sts.*)

Knit 1 row.
Dec 1 st at beg of next row. (*6 sts.*)
Dec 1 st at outer leaf edge on each of next 4 rows. (*2 sts.*)
Bind off.
With RS facing, rejoin A to 8 sts on holder leaving a tail end 8in/20cm long (for attaching leaves to flowers), then k to end.
Knit 1 row.
Dec 1 st at end of next row (outer leaf edge). (*7 sts.*)
Knit 1 row.
Dec 1 st at end of next row. (*6 sts.*)
Dec 1 st at outer leaf edge on each of next 4 rows. (*2 sts.*)
Bind off.
Make 1 more leaf in same way.

SMALL INNER PETALS (MAKE 5)
With size 6 (4mm) needles and B, cast on 5 sts.
Knit 1 row.
Cont in garter st throughout, inc 1 st at

each end of next row (*7 sts.*)
Work even in garter st for 8 rows.
Dec 1 st at each end of next 2 rows. (*3 sts.*)
Next row K2tog, k1.
Next row K2tog, then break off B, thread tail end through rem st, and pull to fasten off.
Make 4 more inner petals in same way.

LARGE OUTER PETALS (MAKE 5)

With size 6 (4mm) needles and B, cast on 7 sts.
Knit 1 row.
Cont in garter st throughout, inc 1 st at each end of next row. (*9 sts.*)
Knit 1 row.
Inc 1 st at each end of next row. (*11 sts.*)
Work even in garter st for 8 rows.
Dec 1 st at each end of next 4 rows. (*3 sts.*)
Next row K2tog, k1.
Next row K2tog, then break off B, thread

tail end through rem st, and pull to fasten off.
Make 4 more outer petals in same way, leaving a 8in/20cm tail end on 2 of them when casting on, to attach flowers to leaves.

STAMENS (MAKE 3)

With size 6 (4mm) needles and C, cast on 8 sts.
Bind off.
Make 2 more stamens in same way.

TO FINISH

Darn in ends of plastic "yarn," but leave ends left long on purpose (on leaves and two of large outer petals).
Take two large petals and overlap them so that one is on top of half of the other, with cast-on edges aligned. Using a sewing needle and matching thread, sew these two petals together along cast-on edge,

slightly gathering base of petals. Continue sewing on remaining three large petals to first two in same way, overlapping each added petal and slightly gathering along base to form a ring of petals. (Leave two long tail ends at back of flower.)
Sew together five small petals in same way to make a ring, then sew to center of ring of large petals.
Sew three stamens to center of water lily, using matching sewing thread, and secure thread to back of flower. Pull petals upward to make water lily look realistic. Underneath flower, knot together two long tail ends from flower and two from leaves, about 1in/2.5cm away from flowers and leaves. Then to form a trailing "root," braid together these tail ends (using two flower tail ends as one strand) and knot together at end. Trim ends close to knot.

HORSE BLANKET

Your horse will delight in this luxurious blanket
whether he's happily grazing or getting ready to run
at Belmont. Make him the envy of his stablemates
by customizing it. Add more squares, his name,
the date he won the Derby (or not), or his colors,
for a unique equine heirloom.

HORSE BLANKET

LEVEL
Intermediate

SIZE
The finished horse blanket measures approximately 31^{1}/2in/80cm wide by 100cm/39^{1}/2in long. (Each individual square measures 8in/20cm.)
Note: If you would like to increase the size of the blanket, add more squares.

MATERIALS
1 x 1^{3}/4oz/50g ball of Jaeger *Matchmaker Merino DK* in each of 9 different colors:
A (charcoal/Charcoal 783), **B** (dark brown/Bison 728), **C** (mid blue/Mariner 629), **D** (violet/Geranium 894), **E** (camel/Syrup 789), **F** (lilac/Dusk 626), **H** (purple/Buddleia 856), **L** (black/Black 728), and **M** (teal/Teal 790)
2 x 1^{3}/4oz/50g balls of Jaeger *Matchmaker Merino DK* in each of 3 different colors:
G (red/Clarice 876), **J** (light green/Sage 857), and **K** (light blue/Marine 914)
Pair of 4mm (US 6) knitting needles

GAUGE
22 sts and 30 rows to 4in/10cm measured over St st using size 6 (4mm) needles.

ABBREVIATIONS
See page 17.

YARN NOTE
The colors listed in the Materials list are there merely to give you an idea for a color combination. Feel free to pick your own selection of 12 different colors to customize the blanket to make it your own. You can use Jaeger *Matchmaker Merino DK*, Rowan *Pure Wool DK*, or any other yarn of the same weight.

CHART NOTE
The charts are worked in St st. When working from the charts, read odd-numbered rows (k rows) from right to left, and even-numbered rows (p rows) from left to right.
When working the chart patterns, use the intarsia method (see page 14), knitting with a separate small ball (or long length) of yarn for each area of color and twisting yarns together on wrong side when changing color to avoid holes.

SQUARE 1—BRIDLE BITS
With size 6 (4mm) needles and M, cast on 44 sts.
Beg with a k row and chart row 1, work in St st following bridle bits chart (see page 132) until all 60 chart rows have been completed. Bind off.

SQUARE 2—PLAIN
With size 6 (4mm) needles and J, cast on 44 sts.
Beg with a k row, work 60 rows in St st. Bind off.

SQUARE 3—RODEO
With size 6 (4mm) needles and D, cast on 44 sts.
Beg with a k row and chart row 1, work in St st following rodeo chart (see page 132) until all 60 chart rows have been completed. Bind off.

SQUARE 4—NARROW STRIPES
With size 6 (4mm) needles and E, cast on 44 sts.
Beg with a k row, work in St st in stripes as follows:
4 rows E, 4 rows G, 4 rows J, 4 rows F.
Rep from * to * twice more.
Cont in St st, work 4 rows E, 4 rows G, and 4 rows J—a total of 60 rows worked

from cast-on edge.
Bind off.

SQUARE 5—BROAD STRIPES
With size 6 (4mm) needles and J, cast on
44 sts.
Beg with a k row, work in St st in stripes
as follows:
6 rows J, 6 rows F, 6 rows K.
Rep from ** to ** twice more.
Cont in St st, work 6 rows J—a total of
60 rows worked from cast-on edge.
Bind off.

SQUARE 6—SMALL CHECKS
With size 6 (4mm) needles and A, cast on
44 sts (if desired, cast on with colors to
match first chart row).
Beg with a k row and chart row 1, work
in St st following small checks chart (see
page 133) until all 60 chart rows have
been completed. Bind off.

SQUARE 7—PLAIN
Work as for square 2, but using K.

SQUARE 8—ROSETTE
With size 6 (4mm) needles and J, cast on
44 sts.
Beg with a k row and chart row 1, work
in St st following rosette chart (see page
133) until all 60 chart rows have been
completed. Bind off.

SQUARE 9—HORSESHOE
With size 6 (4mm) needles and K, cast on
44 sts.
Beg with a k row and chart row 1, work
in St st following horseshoe chart (see
page 134) until all 60 chart rows have
been completed. Bind off.

SQUARE 10—PLAIN
Work as for square 2, but using M.

SQUARE 11—BRIDLE BITS
Work as for square 1, but using B for
background instead of M.

SQUARE 12—PLAIN
Work as for square 2, but using C.

SQUARE 13—PLAIN
Work as for square 2, but using B.

SQUARE 14—BIG CHECKS
With size 6 (4mm) needles and K, cast on
44 sts (if desired, cast on with colors to
match first chart row).
Beg with a k row and chart row 1, work
in St st following big checks chart (see
page 134) until all 60 chart rows have
been completed. Bind off.

SQUARE 15—NAME
With size 6 (4mm) needles and J, cast on
44 sts.
Beg with a k row and chart row 1,
work in St st following name chart (see
Note below) until all 60 chart rows have
been completed.
Bind off.
(Note: Use chart on page 135, or if
desired, insert your own horse's name,
using alphabet chart on page 140.)

SQUARE 16—RODEO
Work as for square 3, but using F for
background instead of D.

SQUARE 17—SPOTS
With size 6 (4mm) needles and H, cast on
44 sts.
Beg with a k row and chart row 1,
work in St st following spots chart (see
page 135) until all 60 chart rows have
been completed.
Bind off.

SQUARE 18—PLAIN
Work as for square 2, but using F.

SQUARE 19—SPOTS
Work as for square 17, but using D for
background and M for spots.

SQUARE 20—PLAIN
Work as for square 2, but using G.

TO FINISH
Block and press all 20 squares lightly
on wrong side, following instructions on
yarn label.

Lay out squares on floor to make a
patchwork four squares wide by five
squares long. Make your own arrangement
to customize your blanket; or arrange as
for blanket pictured—using squares 1–4
(from left to right) for the top row, squares
5–8 (from left to right) for the second row
down, and so on. (Note: Position the
rodeo and rosette in top half of blanket
upside down so that when blanket is on
horse, they will be upright.)
To sew squares together, take the first two
squares from a vertical row of squares and
with right sides together, sew them together
along cast-on/bound-off edges, using
overcast stitch and a yarn that matches
one of the squares.
Sew together all five squares in the first
vertical row.
Then sew together remaining vertical rows
(of five squares each) in same way.
Pin and sew all these four strips together.
Press again.

MOUSE MAT FOR **CAT**

An absolutely vital lounging accessory for cats.
Quick to knit, yet stylish to have about the house,
it implies tremendous bravery with the giant mouse
skin while also keeping cat hairs off the furniture.

MOUSE MAT FOR **CAT**

LEVEL
Easy

SIZE
The finished mouse mat measures approximately 15³/₄in/40cm wide across the body and 29¹/₂in/75cm long from nose to tail.
Note: If your cat is enormous, you can make the mat bigger by adding more stitches and rows in the center.

MATERIALS
2 x 3¹/₂oz/100g balls of Rowan *Scottish Tweed Chunky* in main color **MC**, for mat and back of ears
Small amount of Rowan *Scottish Tweed Chunky* in a contrasting color **A**, for inside of ears, nose, and whiskers
Small amount of double-knitting-weight yarn that matches MC, for sewing ear fronts to ear backs
Pair of size 11 (8mm) knitting needles
2 black buttons, for eyes
Crochet hook, for attaching whiskers

GAUGE
11 sts and 19 rows to 4in/10cm measured over garter st using size 11 (8mm) needles.

ABBREVIATIONS
See page 17.

TO MAKE MOUSE MAT
The whole body and tail of mouse mat is knitted in garter st, starting at tail end.

Shape tail
With size 11 (8mm) needles and MC, cast on 2 sts.
Work 12 rows in garter st (knit every row).
Cont in garter st throughout, inc 1 st at each end of next row. *(4 sts.)*
Work even for 11 rows.
Inc 1 st at each end of next row. *(6 sts.)*
Work even for 11 rows.

Begin body
Cast on 12 sts at end of next 2 rows. *(30 sts.)*
Work even for 1 row.

Inc 1 st at each end of next 9 rows. *(48 sts.)*
Work even for 2 rows.

Shape back legs
**Cast on 10 sts at end of next 2 rows. *(68 sts.)*
Inc 1 st at each end of next 3 rows. *(74 sts.)*
Work even for 4 rows.
Dec 1 st at each end of next 3 rows. *(68 sts.)*
Bind off 11 sts at beg of next 2 rows. *(46 sts.)*******
Work even for 36 rows.

Shape front legs
Rep from ****** to ****** once more.

Work even for 1 row. *(44 sts.)*

Shape neck and head
Bind off 5 sts at beg of next 2 rows. *(34 sts.)*
Bind off 4 sts at beg of next 2 rows. *(26 sts.)*
Bind off 2 sts at beg of next 2 rows. *(22 sts.)*
Work even for 4 rows.
Dec 1 st at each end of next row and then at each end of 2 foll 4th rows. *(16 sts.)*
Dec 1 st at each end of 3 foll alt rows. *(10 sts.)*
Dec 1 st at each end of next 4 rows. *(2 sts.)*
Work even for 2 rows.
Next row K2tog, then break off yarn,

thread tail end through rem st, and pull to fasten off.

EAR BACKS (MAKE 2)
With size 11 (8mm) needles and MC, cast on 6 sts.
Beg with a k row, work 2 rows in St st, ending with a p row.
Cont in St st throughout, inc 1 st at each end of next row. *(8 sts.)*
Work even for 5 rows, ending with a p row.
Dec 1 st at each end of next row and then at each end of foll alt row, ending with a k row. *(4 sts.)*
Work even for 1 row.
Bind off.
Make a second ear back in same way.

EAR FRONTS (MAKE 2)
With size 11 (8mm) needles and A, cast on 5 sts.
Work 2 rows in garter st.
Cont in garter st throughout, inc 1 st at each end of next row. *(7 sts.)*
Work even for 5 rows
Dec 1 st at each end of next row and then at each end of foll alt row. *(3 sts.)*
Work even for 1 row.
Bind off.
Make a second ear front in same way.

TO FINISH
Using double-knitting yarn, sew fronts of ears to backs. Sew ears to mouse's head, parallel to front legs and approximately 3in/7.5cm apart. Lightly press ear backs on wrong side, following instructions on yarn label and avoiding garter st.

Nose, whiskers, and eyes
Using a blunt-ended yarn needle and A, sew tip of head over and over to make nose. For whiskers, cut eight 4in/10cm lengths of A. Fold one length in half and use a crochet hook to pull looped end through edge of mat 1/4in/6mm from nose; pull ends of yarn through loop and tighten. Attach three more lengths of yarn A along edge of head and about 1/2in/12mm apart, working away from nose. Attach four whiskers on other side of nose in same way.
Sew on two buttons for eyes, about 2in/5cm apart and 1 1/2in/4cm from ears.

PARTY **DOG** COLLARS

Dress up your dog for a special occasion in a party dog collar. The covers are slipped onto the dog's collar and then popped over its head. There are five designs to choose from: a majestic ruffle, a chic tapestry of flowers, dashing spots, a Hell's Angel collar for the rottweiler in your dog, or perhaps a seductive garland of flowers.

RUFFLE **DOG** COLLAR

LEVEL
Easy

SIZES
The finished collar cover measures approximately 1½in/4cm wide for all sizes, and the lengths are as follows:

Extra-extra small—to fit collar size 10in/25cm
Extra small—to fit collar size 12in/30.5cm
Small—to fit collar size 14in/35.5cm
Medium—to fit collar size 16in/40.5cm
Large—to fit collar size 18in/45.5cm
Extra large—to fit collar size 20in/50.5cm

MATERIALS
1 (1: 2: 2: 2: 2) x 1¾oz/50g balls of of Jaeger *Matchmaker Merino 4-Ply* in main color **MC**
1 x ⅞oz/25g ball of Rowan *Kidsilk Haze* in a contrasting color **A**
Pair of size 3 (3.25mm) knitting needles

GAUGE
28 sts and 36 rows to 4in/10cm measured over St st using size 3 (3.25mm) needles and MC.

ABBREVIATIONS
See page 17

TO MAKE COLLAR COVER
With size 3 (3.25mm) needles and MC, cast on 24 sts.
Work 2 rows in garter st (knit every row).
Beg St st section as follows:
1st row (RS) K6, p1, k17.
2nd row P17, k1, p6.
Rep last 2 rows until collar cover measures 9 (11: 13: 15: 17: 19)in/22.5 (28: 33: 38: 43: 48)cm from cast-on edge, ending with a WS row.
Work 2 rows in garter st, ending with a WS row.
Next row (RS) Bind off first 12 sts knitwise, k to end. *(12 sts.)*
Work 10 rows in garter st.
Bind off knitwise.

RUFFLE
With size 3 (3.25mm) needles and A, cast on 165 (195: 231: 267: 306: 363) sts.
Work 2 rows in garter st (knit every row).
Break off A, change to MC, and cont as follows:
Work 12 rows in garter st.
Next row *K3tog; rep from * to end. *(55 (65: 77: 89: 102: 121) sts.)*
Work 2 rows in garter st.
Next row [K1, p1, k1] all into each st to end (to inc twice into each st). *(165 (195: 231: 267: 306: 363) sts.)*
Work 12 rows in garter st.
Break off MC, change to A, and cont as follows:

Work 2 rows in garter st.
Bind off knitwise.

TO FINISH
Press collar cover lightly on wrong side, following instructions on yarn label.
With wrong side of ruffle facing right side of collar cover, sew ruffle to collar cover, stitching along center of ruffle and through line of rev St st on collar cover.
Fold collar cover in half lengthwise and sew long side edges together to form a tube.
Sew bound-off edge of collar cover to corresponding section of cast-on edge.
Slip cover onto dog's collar, positioning buckle over garter st section.

FLORAL **DOG** COLLAR

LEVEL
Intermediate

SIZES
The finished collar cover measures approximately 4cm/1¹/₂in wide for all sizes, and the lengths are as follows:
Extra small—to fit collar size 12in/30.5cm
Small—to fit collar size 14in/35.5cm
Medium—to fit collar size 16in/40.5cm
Large—to fit collar size 18in/45.5cm
Extra large—to fit collar size 20in/50.5cm

MATERIALS
1 x 1³/₄oz/50g ball of Jaeger *Matchmaker Merino 4-Ply* in main color **MC** (charcoal/Anthracite 217), for background
Small amount of Jaeger *Matchmaker Merino 4-Ply* in **A** (light blue/Dewberry), for flower petal motifs
Small amount of Rowan *Scottish Tweed 4-Ply* in each of **B** (blue-green/Sea Green 006), **C** (lavender/Lavender 005), and **D** (green/Apple 015), for leaf motifs and flower centers
Pair of size 3 (3.25mm) knitting needles

GAUGE
28 sts and 36 rows to 4in/10cm measured over St st using size 3 (3.25mm) needles and MC.
31 rows to 4in/10cm measured over chart patt using size 3 (3.25mm) needles.

ABBREVIATIONS
See page 17.

CHART NOTE
The chart is worked in St st. When working from the chart, read odd-numbered rows (k rows) from right to left, and even-numbered rows (p rows) from left to right. When working the chart pattern, use the intarsia method (see page 14), knitting with a separate small ball (or long length) of yarn for each area of color and twisting yarns together on wrong side when changing color to avoid holes.

TO MAKE COLLAR COVER
With size 3 (3.25mm) needles and MC, cast on 24 sts.

Work 2 rows in garter st (knit every row).
Beg with a k row, work 0 (2: 10: 20: 28) rows in St st, ending with a WS row.
Beg with a k row and chart row 1, work in St st foll chart (see page 136) until all 98 chart rows have been completed, ending with a p row.
Using MC only and cont in St st, work 0 (2: 10: 20: 28 rows), ending with a p row—collar cover measures 11 (13: 15: 17: 19)in/28 (33: 38: 43: 48)cm from cast-on edge.
Work 2 rows in garter stitch, ending with a WS row.
Next row (RS) Bind off first 12 sts knitwise,

k to end. *(12 sts.)*
Work 10 rows in garter st.
Bind off knitwise.

TO FINISH
Block and press lightly on wrong side, following instructions on yarn label.
Fold collar cover in half lengthwise with right sides together and sew long side edges together to form a tube. Turn right side out and press again.
Sew bound-off edge of collar cover to corresponding section of cast-on edge.
Slip cover onto dog's collar, positioning buckle over garter st section.

S P O T   **D O G**   C O L L A R

LEVEL
Easy

SIZES
The finished collar cover measures approximately 1 1/2in/4cm wide for all sizes, and the lengths are as follows:

Extra-extra small—to fit collar size 10in/25cm
Extra small—to fit collar size 12in/30.5cm
Small—to fit collar size 14in/35.5cm
Medium—to fit collar size 16in/40.5cm
Large—to fit collar size 18in/45.5cm
Extra large—to fit collar size 20in/50.5cm

MATERIALS
1 x 1 3/4oz/50g ball of Jaeger *Matchmaker Merino 4-Ply* (or Rowan *Scottish Tweed 4-Ply*) in main color **MC**, for background
Small amount of Jaeger *Matchmaker Merino 4-Ply* (or Rowan *Scottish Tweed 4-Ply*) in each of 5 (5: 5: 5: 5: 6) contrasting colors, for spot motifs
Pair of size 3 (3.25mm) knitting needles

GAUGE
28 sts and 36 rows to 4in/10cm measured over St st using size 3 (3.25mm) needles and MC.

ABBREVIATIONS
See page 17.

CHART NOTE
The chart is worked in St st. When working from the chart, read odd-numbered rows (k rows) from right to left, and even-numbered rows (p rows) from left to right. When working the chart pattern, use the intarsia method (see page 14), knitting with a separate small ball (or long length) of yarn for each area of color and twisting yarns together on wrong side when changing color to avoid holes.

TO MAKE COLLAR COVER
With size 3 (3.25mm) needles and MC, cast on 24 sts.
Work 2 rows in garter st (knit every row).

Beg with a k row, work 4 rows in St st, ending with a p row.
Beg with a k row and chart row 1, work in St st foll chart (see page 136) until all 16 chart rows have been completed, using desired contrasting color for first spot motif.
Cont as set, repeating chart rows 1–16 and using desired random contrasting colors for spot motifs, until collar cover measures approximately 9 (11: 13: 15: 17: 19)in/22.5 (28: 33: 38: 43: 48)cm from cast-on edge and ending with a chart row 8 (a p row).
Cont with MC only, work 2 rows in garter st, ending with a WS row.

Next row (RS) Bind off first 12 sts knitwise, k to end. *(12 sts.)*
Work 10 rows in garter st.
Bind off knitwise.

TO FINISH
Block and press lightly on wrong side, following instructions on yarn label.
Fold collar cover in half lengthwise with right sides together and sew long side edges together to form a tube. Turn right side out and press again.
Sew bound-off edge of collar cover to corresponding section of cast-on edge.
Slip cover onto dog's collar, positioning buckle over garter st section.

HELL'S ANGEL **DOG** COLLAR

LEVEL
Intermediate

SIZES
The finished collar cover measures approximately 1¹/₂in/4cm wide for all sizes, and the lengths are as follows:
Small—to fit collar size 14in/35.5cm
Medium—to fit collar size 16in/40.5cm
Large—to fit collar size 18in/45.5cm
Extra large—to fit collar size 20in/50.5cm

MATERIALS
1 x 1³/₄oz/50g ball of Rowan *4-Ply Soft* in main color **MC** (black/Black 383), for background
Small amount of Twilleys *Goldfingering* in **A** (gold/Gold 002), for lettering and part of motif
Small amount of Rowan *4-Ply Soft* in each of **B** (white/Nippy 376) and **C** (red/Honk 374), for motifs
Pair of size 3 (3.25mm) knitting needles

GAUGE
28 sts and 36 rows to 4in/10cm measured over St st using size 3 (3.25mm) needles and MC.

ABBREVIATIONS
See page 17.

CHART NOTE
The chart is worked in St st. When working from the chart, read odd-numbered rows (k rows) from right to left, and even-numbered rows (p rows) from left to right. When working the chart pattern, use the intarsia method (see page 14), knitting with a separate small ball (or long length) of yarn for each area of color and twisting yarns together on wrong side when changing color to avoid holes.

TO MAKE COLLAR COVER
With size 3 (3.25mm) needles and MC, cast on 24 sts.

Work 2 rows in garter st (knit every row).
Beg with a k row, work 2 (8: 16: 26) rows in St st, ending with a p row.
Beg with a k row and chart row 1, work in St st foll chart (see page 136) until all 106 chart rows have been completed, ending with a p row.
Using MC only and cont in St st, work until collar cover measures 13 (15: 17: 19)in/ 33 (38: 43: 48)cm from cast-on edge, ending with a p row.
Work 2 rows in garter stitch, ending with a WS row.
Next row (RS) Bind off first 12 sts knitwise, k to end. *(12 sts.)*

Work 10 rows in garter st.
Bind off knitwise.

TO FINISH
Block and press lightly on wrong side, following instructions on yarn label.
Fold collar cover in half lengthwise with right sides together and sew long side edges together to form a tube. Turn right side out and press again.
Sew bound-off edge of collar cover to corresponding section of cast-on edge.
Slip cover onto dog's collar, positioning buckle over garter st section.

GARLAND **DOG** COLLAR

LEVEL
Intermediate

SIZES
The finished collar cover measures approximately 1¹/₂in/4cm wide for all sizes, and the lengths are as follows:

Extra-extra small—to fit collar size 10in/25cm
Extra-small—to fit collar size 12in/30.5cm
Small—to fit collar size 14in/35.5cm
Medium—to fit collar size 16in/40.5cm
Large—to fit collar size 18in/45.5cm
Extra-large—to fit collar size 20in/50.5cm

MATERIALS
1 x 1³/₄oz/50g ball of Jaeger *Matchmaker Merino 4-Ply* in main color **MC** (mustard/Gold 756)
1 x ⁷/₈oz/25g ball of Rowan *Scottish Tweed 4-Ply* each in 6 different colors:
A (purple/Thistle 016), **B** (maroon/Claret 013), **C** (blue-green/Sea Green 006), **D** (rust/Rust 009), **E** (lavender/Lavender 005), and **F** (green/Apple 015), OR any scraps of leftover fine-weight yarn at hand
Pair of size 3 (3.25mm) knitting needles

GAUGE
28 sts and 36 rows to 4in/10cm measured over St st using size 3 (3.25mm) needles and MC.

ABBREVIATIONS
See page 17.

TO MAKE COLLAR COVER
With size 3 (3.25mm) needles and MC, cast on 24 sts.
Work 2 rows in garter st (knit every row).
Beg with a k row, work in St st until collar cover measures 9 (11: 13: 15: 17: 19)in/ 22.5 (28: 33: 38: 43: 48)cm from cast-on edge, ending with a p row.
Work 2 rows in garter st, ending with a WS row.
Next row (RS) Bind off first 12 sts knitwise, k to end. *(12 sts.)*
Work 10 rows in garter st.
Bind off knitwise.

FLOWER 1
With size 3 (3.25mm) needles and A, cast on 40 sts.
Knit 1 row.

First petal
Next row (RS) K10, then turn, leaving rem sts unworked.
Working on these 10 sts only, make first petal as follows:
Purl 1 row.
Cont in St st throughout, inc 1 st at each end of next row and at each end of foll alt row, ending with a k row. *(14 sts.)*

Purl 1 row.
Dec 1 st at each end of next row and at each end of every foll alt row until 2 sts rem, ending with a k row.
Next row (WS) P2tog, then break off yarn, thread tail end through rem st, and pull tight to fasten off.

Second petal
With RS facing, return to sts left unworked and using D, k10, then turn, leaving rem sts unworked.
Working on these 10 sts only, make second petal as follows:

70

Knit 1 row.
Cont in garter st throughout, inc 1 st at each end of next row and at each end of foll alt row. *(14 sts.)*
Knit 1 row.
Dec 1 st at each end of next row and at each end of every foll alt row until 2 sts rem.
Next row K2tog, then break off yarn, thread tail end through rem st, and pull tight to fasten off.

Third and fourth petals
Cont as set, working third petal in St st in A as for first petal, and fourth (final) petal in garter st in D as for second petal.

FLOWER 2
With size 3 (3.25mm) needles and C, cast on 32 sts.
Knit 1 row.

First petal
Next row (RS) K10, then turn, leaving rem sts unworked.
Working on these 10 sts only, make first petal as follows:
Cont in garter st throughout, inc 1 st at each end of next row and at each end of foll alt row. *(14 sts.)*
Dec 1 st at each end of next row and at each end of every foll alt row until 2 sts rem.
Next row K2tog, then break off yarn, thread tail end through rem st, and pull tight to fasten off.

Second petal
With RS facing, return to sts left unworked and using D, k6, then turn, leaving rem sts unworked.
Working on these 6 sts only, make second petal as follows:
Purl 1 row.
Cont in St st throughout, inc 1 st at each end of next row and at each end of 2 foll alt rows, ending with a k row. *(12 sts.)*

Purl 1 row.
Work 2 rows in St st, ending with a p row.
Dec 1 st at each end of next row and at each end of every foll alt row until 2 sts rem, ending with a k row.
Next row (WS) P2tog, then break off yarn, thread tail end through rem st, and pull tight to fasten off.

Third and fourth petals
Cont as set, working third petal in garter st in C across 10 sts as for first petal, and fourth (final) petal in St st in D across 6 sts as for second petal.

STAMENS (MAKE 6)
With size 3 (3.25mm) needles and E, cast on 14 sts.
Bind off knitwise.
Make 5 more stamens in same way.
(If you want stamens to look particularly botanical, sew over and over end of each stamen to make the stigma, using F.)

LEAVES (MAKE 3)
With size 3 (3.25mm) needles and F, cast on 5 sts.
1st row (RS) *K1, k into front and back of next st—called *inc into next st*; rep from * once more, k1. *(7 sts.)*
2nd row and all foll WS rows Purl to end.
3rd row K2, inc into next st, k1, inc into next st, k2. *(9 sts.)*
5th row K3, inc into next st, k1, inc into next st, k3. *(11 sts.)*
7th row K4, inc into next st, k1, inc into next st, k4. *(13 sts.)*
9th row K5, inc into next st, k1 inc into next st, k5. *(15 sts.)*
11th row K to end.
13th row K1, k2tog, k9, k2tog, k1. *(13 sts.)*
15th row K1, k2tog, k7, k2tog, k1. *(11 sts.)*
17th row K1, k2tog, k5, k2tog, k1. *(9 sts.)*

19th row K1, k2tog, k3, k2tog, k1. *(7 sts.)*
21st row K1, k2tog, k1, k2tog, k1. *(5 sts.)*
Bind off purlwise.

PETALS (MAKE 2)
With size 3 (3.25mm) needles and B, cast on 4 sts.
Working in garter st throughout, inc 1 st at each end of first row and at each end of 3 foll alt rows. *(12 sts.)*
Knit 1 row.
Dec 1 st at each end of next row and at each end of 4 foll alt rows. *(2 sts.)*
Knit 1 row.
Next row (RS) K2tog, then break off yarn, thread tail end through rem st, and pull tight to fasten off.
Make second petal in same way.

TO FINISH
Press collar cover, leaves, and petals lightly on wrong side, following instructions on yarn label.
Fold collar cover in half lengthwise with right sides together and sew long side edges together to form a tube. Turn right side out and press again.

Add petals and leaves
Curl flower 1 around on itself and sew together at base so that it forms a four-petaled flower. Sew three stamens to center of flower.
Sew flower 2 together in same way.
Arrange flowers, leaves, and petals at center of collar as shown, positioning bound-off end of leaves and cast-on end of petals under flowers. Sew in place as arranged.
Sew bound-off edge of collar cover to corresponding section of cast-on edge.
Slip cover onto dog's collar, positioning buckle over garter st section.

TORTOISE HIBERNATION TENT

Why should a tortoise spend six months a year living in a cardboard box? At last, a chance to knit a magnificent tent for your tortoise to winter in. Knitted in subtle colors, the tent will look gorgeous in most places, be it a garden shed or a cellar, but be sure to keep it dry. For the remaining six months, you could lend the tent to your cat or small dog, or use it for a teddy bear's camping trip.

TORTOISE HIBERNATION TENT

LEVEL
Knitted tent: Easy
Wooden tent frame: Intermediate

SIZE
The finished tent measures approximately 14in/35cm wide by 19in/48cm long by 15in/37.5cm tall.

MATERIALS
Knitted tent
2 x 1¾oz/50g balls of Jaeger *Matchmaker Merino DK* in **A** (mid blue/Mariner 629), for base of tent
2 x 1¾oz/50g balls of Jaeger *Matchmaker Merino DK* in **B** (lilac/Dusk 626), for one side of tent
2 x 1¾oz/50g balls of Jaeger *Matchmaker Merino DK* in **C** (light sea blue/Marine 914), for one side of tent
1 x 1¾oz/50g ball of Jaeger *Matchmaker Merino DK* in **D** (dark green/Loden 730), for back of tent
1 x 1¾oz/50g ball of Jaeger *Matchmaker Merino DK* in **E** (light green/Sage 857), for front of tent
Pair of size 6 (4mm) knitting needles

Wooden tent frame
3 lengths of wooden doweling, each ¼in/6mm in diameter and approximately 51cm/20in long (to fit along two sides of base of tent and along top of tent)
2 lengths of wooden doweling, each ¼in/6mm in diameter and approximately 40.5cm/16in long (to fit along front and back of base of tent)
4 lengths of wooden doweling, each ¼in/6mm in diameter and approximately 48.5cm/19in long (to form A-shape frames at front and back of tent)
Jute twine or string (a slightly rough version will hold better)
Strong adhesive tape, for binding frame joints

GAUGE
22 sts and 30 rows to 4in/10cm measured over St st using size 6 (4mm) needles.

ABBREVIATIONS
See page 17.

SPECIAL NOTE
Do not cut the doweling into pieces for the frame until you have finished knitting the tent. Because of variable gauges you may need to adjust the length of the wooden rods to fit the size of the finished knitting.

KNITTED TENT

BASE OF TENT

With size 6 (4mm) needles and A, cast on 106 sts.
1st row (RS) K to end.
2nd row K5, p to end.
Rep last 2 rows (working in St st with a 5-st border in garter st along tent front edge as set) until base measures 14in/35cm from cast-on edge (approximately 104 rows in total), ending with a p row.
Bind off.

LONG SIDE OF TENT (MAKE 2)

With size 6 (4mm) needles and B, cast on 106 sts.
Beg with a k row, work in St st until side measures 15in/37.5cm from cast-on edge (approximately 112 rows in total), ending with a p row.
Bind off.
Make second side in same way, but using C.

BACK OF TENT

With size 6 (4mm) needles and D, cast on 80 sts.
Beg with a k row, work 2 rows in St st, ending with a p row.
Cont in St st throughout, dec 1 st at each end of next row and then at each end of every foll 3rd row until 2 sts rem (118 rows in total), ending with a p row.
Next row K2tog, then break off D, thread tail end through rem st, and pull tight to fasten off.

RIGHT FRONT OF TENT

With size 6 (4mm) needles and E, cast on 41 sts.
Work 2 rows in garter st (knit every row).
Cont in garter st, dec 1 st at beg of next row. (39 sts.)
Work 1 row more in garter st.
Next row (RS) K to end.
Next row K5, p to last 2 sts, p2tog. (37 sts.)
Next row K to end.
Next row K5, p to end.
Cont as set, working in St st with a 5-st border in garter st along left edge, **and at the same time** dec 1 st at beg of next row and at same edge (edge without border) on every foll 3rd row until 2 sts rem, ending with a p row.
Next row K2tog, then break off E, thread tail end through rem st, and pull tight to fasten off.

LEFT FRONT OF TENT

With size 6 (4mm) needles and E, cast on 41 sts.
Work 2 rows in garter st (knit every row).
Cont in garter st, dec 1 st at end of next row. (39 sts.)
Work 1 row more in garter st.
Next row (RS) K to end.
Next row P2tog, p to last 5 sts, k5. (37 sts.)
Next row K to end.
Next row P to last 5 sts, k5.
Cont as set, working in St st with a 5-st border in garter st along right edge, **and at the same time** dec 1 st at end of next row and at same edge (edge without border) on every foll 3rd row until 2 sts rem, ending with a p row.
Next row K2tog, then break off E, thread tail end through rem st, and pull tight to fasten off.

FLAGS

With size 6 (4mm) needles and A, cast on 116 sts.
Knit 1 row.
Next row (RS) Bind off first 19 sts knitwise, k until there are 8 sts on right needle, then turn, leaving rem sts unworked.
Working on these 8 sts only, drop A and make first flag as follows.
**Using B for flag, work 7 rows in garter st (knit every row).
Cont in garter st for flag throughout, dec 1 st at each end of next row. (6 sts.)
Work 7 rows in garter st.
Dec 1 st at each end of next row. (4 sts.)
Work 7 rows in garter st.
Next row [K2tog] twice. (2 sts.)
Work 1 row in garter st.
Next row K2tog, then break off flag yarn, thread tail end through rem st, and pull tight to fasten off.**
***With RS facing, return to sts left unworked and using A, bind off 2 sts knitwise, k until there are 8 sts on right needle, then turn, leaving rem sts unworked.
Working on these 8 sts only, drop A and make next flag as for first flag from ** to ** but using C.***
Rep from *** to *** 6 times more, using D for 3rd flag, E for 4th flag, B for 5th flag, C for for 6th flag, D for 7th flag, and E for 8th flag.
With RS facing, return to sts left unworked and using A, bind off rem sts knitwise.

TO FINISH

Block and press tent pieces lightly on wrong side, following instructions on yarn label.
With right sides together, sew cast-on edge of tent base to cast-on edge of side worked in B, and sew bound-off edge of tent base to cast-on edge of side worked in C. Then sew bound-off edges of sides together at top to form a triangular shape. Sew back of tent to back of base (end without garter st border) and sides, leaving a 2.5cm/1in opening at top for wooden rod to stick out of.
Sew fronts together for 1in/2.5cm at center top, 1in/2.5cm below top edge, so leaving a split at apex for rod.

Cords

Make six cords as follows:
Using E, cut two strands of yarn each 14³/4in/37.5cm long. Holding two strands together, knot each end. Ask a friend to hold one end (or tie one end to a door handle). Insert a pencil in front of knot between two strands at each end and have person at each end twist pencil clockwise until strands are very tightly twisted. Fold twisted yarn in half, give it a slight pull, then allow it to twist up on itself. Smooth out any unevenness, working away from knots. Knot together knotted end, and cut off original two knots. Sew folded (unknotted) end of each cord to center of borders on tent fronts, stitching three to each front and spacing them evenly apart.

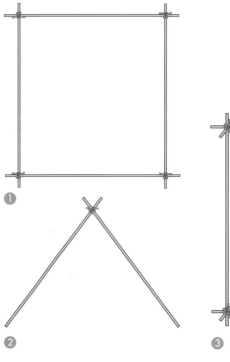

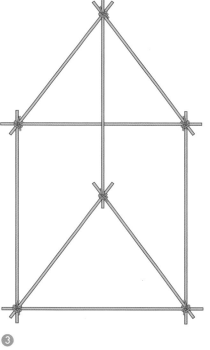

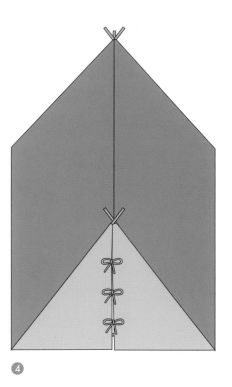

WOODEN TENT FRAME

TO CUT FRAME PIECES
Check that the tent width, length, and height match the sizes given at the beginning of the pattern, and adjust the doweling lengths given in the Materials list if necessary.
Next, cut nine doweling pieces to the correct lengths with a saw, and gently sand the ends.

TO ASSEMBLE FRAME
Cut the twine into 12in/30.5cm lengths.
(Fig 1) Starting with the base-frame of the tent, use twine to bind together two 20in/51cm lengths of doweling (to fit along the sides of the tent base) with two 16in/40.5cm lengths (to fit along the front and back of the tent base). To bind the rods together, wrap the twine over

and around the "joint," leaving about 1/2in/12mm of the rods protruding. Once the joint is fairly secure, knot the twine. (When the tent is finished, the structure will be more stable.)
(Fig 2) Take two 19in/48.5cm lengths of doweling and bind them together at the top to form an A-shape for the back of the tent, leaving about 2in/5cm above the binding (as on a wigwam) to tie the flags onto.
(Fig 3) Place the bottom of the A-shape on the inside of the back corners of the base-frame and bind in place with twine. Make a second A-shape frame for the front of the tent, using the remaining two 19in/48.5cm lengths of doweling; then bind it to the base-frame.
Wrap the tape around the four joints at the base of the tent to stop the rods from sliding.

Rest the remaining 20in/51cm length of doweling in the crosses at the top of A-shapes, and bind in place at each end using twine only.

TO SET UP TENT
(Fig 4) Carefully slip the tent over the frame, allowing the crossed points of doweling to pass through the openings at the two top corners of the tent.
To secure the flags to the tent, tie one end to the top of left front rod and tie the other end to right back rod.
Fill the tent with straw and introduce your tortoise.

ANTI-FIREWORK **DOG** BALACLAVA

This is a really useful item for all those dogs that find fireworks a misery. Just slip on the balaclava, with extra earmuff protection, and your dog's ears are muffled from the terrifying sounds. As you can see they also cut quite a dash.

ANTI-FIREWORK **DOG** BALACLAVA

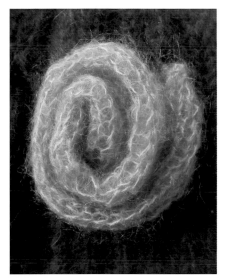

LEVEL
Easy

SIZES
Small—to fit small to medium-size dog
The finished small size measures
approximately 9¹/₂in/24cm around
the neck and 10¹/₂in/26.5cm long
unstretched.
Large—to fit medium-size to large dog
The finished large size measures
approximately 12¹/₂in/32cm around
the neck and 12in/30.5cm long
unstretched.
Note: The ribbed balaclava is stretchy
and will fit easily over the dog's head;
when on the dog, the circumference
will be wider and the length shorter
than when unstretched.

MATERIALS
1 (2) x 1³/₄oz/50g ball of Rowan
Kid Classic in main color **MC**,
for balaclava
Small amount of Rowan *Kidsilk Haze*
in a contrasting color **A**, for earmuffs
Pair of size 8 (5mm) knitting needles

GAUGE
18–19 sts and 23–25 rows to
4in/10cm measured over St st
using size 8 (5mm) knitting needles
and MC.

ABBREVIATIONS
See page 17.

TO MAKE BALACLAVA
With size 8 (5mm) needles and MC,
cast on 62 (82) sts.
Beg k2, p2 rib as follows:
1st rib row (RS) *K2, p2; rep from * to
last 2 sts, k2.
2nd rib row *P2, k2; rep from * to last
2 sts, p2.
(Last 2 rows are repeated to form k2,
p2 rib patt.)
Work 38 (44) rows more in k2, p2 rib,
ending with a WS row.

Divide for front opening
Keeping rib patt correct as set, divide for
opening on next row as follows:
Next row (RS) Work first 25 (32) sts in
rib and slip these sts onto a st holder, then
bind off next 12 (18) sts in rib, work in
rib to end.
Working on these 25 (32) sts only, cont
as follows:
Work 15 (19) rows in rib, ending with
a WS row.
Break off MC and leave these sts on
a spare needle.
With WS facing, rejoin MC to sts on
holder and work in rib to end.
Work 14 (18) rows in rib, ending with
a WS row.
Next row (RS) Work in rib across 25 (32)
on needle, cast on 12 (18) sts onto right-
hand needle, then work in rib across 25
(32) sts on spare needle. *(62 (82) sts.)*
Work 1 row in rib.

Shape top
Next row (RS) *K6, k2tog; rep from * to
last 6 (2) sts, k6 (2). *(55 (72) sts.)*

Purl 1 row.
Next row *K5, k2tog; rep from * to last
6 (2) sts, k6 (2). *(48 (62) sts.)*
Purl 1 row.
Next row *K4, k2tog; rep from * to last
6 (2) sts, k6 (2). *(41 (52) sts.)*
Purl 1 row.
Next row *K3, k2tog; rep from * to last
6 (2) sts, k6 (2). *(34 (42) sts.)*
Purl 1 row.
Next row *K2, k2tog; rep from * to last
6 (2) sts, k6 (2). *(27 (32) sts.)*
Purl 1 row.
Next row [K2tog] 13 (16) times, k1 (0).
(14 (16) sts.)
Next row [P2tog] 7 (8) times. *(7 (8) sts.)*
Next row [K2tog] 3 (4) times, k1 (0).
(4 sts.)
Next row [P2tog] twice. *(2 sts.)*
Next row K2tog, then break off MC,
thread tail end through rem st, and pull
tight to fasten off.

EARMUFFS (MAKE 2)
With size 8 (5mm) needles and A, cast on
10 sts.
Beg with a k row, work in St st until strip
measures 10in/25cm from cast-on edge,
ending with a WS row.
Bind off, leaving a long tail end.

TO FINISH
Press balaclava very lightly on WS,
following instructions on yarn label.
Sew side edges of balaclava together
to form back seam.

Earmuffs
Do not press earmuff strips, but allow them
to curl in along side edges to form a long
tube shape. Starting at cast-on end, curl
each strip into a spiraling circle (like a
snail), about 2¹/₂in/6.5cm in diameter.
Thread long tail end onto a blunt-ended
yarn needle and secure circle shape by
passing needle through circle spirals from
one edge of circle to opposite edge.
Sew one earmuff to each side of balaclava,
level with center of front opening.

PARAKEET BLANKET

For the discerning bird, a knitted cage cover. As they sit on their perch and look up they will have the illusion that they are gazing up at the sky through a canopy of leaves. They may, of course, not notice this feature, but as they sleep you will have the added bonus of a beautiful piece of knitting to admire.

PARAKEET BLANKET

LEVEL
Intermediate

SIZE
The finished blanket measures approximately 23¼in/59cm wide by 54in/137cm long.
Note: To make the blanket longer, you can add rows in MC before beginning the chart and the same number of rows in MC after completing the chart. To make the blanket wider, add the same number of stitches to each side of chart in MC.

MATERIALS
5 x 1¾oz/50g balls of Jaeger *Matchmaker Merino DK* in main color **MC** (dark olive), for borders and outer background
3 x 1¾oz/50g ball of Jaeger *Matchmaker Merino DK* in **E** (pale blue), for center background
1 x 1¾oz/50g ball of Jaeger *Matchmaker Merino DK* in each of **A** (mid green), **B** (pale lime green), **C** (light green), **D** (dark green), and **F** (brown), for leaf motifs
Pair of size 6 (4mm) knitting needles

GAUGE
22 sts and 30 rows to 4in/10cm measured over St st using size 6 (4mm) needles.

ABBREVIATIONS
See page 17.

CHART NOTE
The chart is worked in St st. When working from the chart, read odd-numbered rows (k rows) from right to left, and even-numbered rows (p rows) from left to right. When working the chart pattern, use the intarsia method (see page 14), knitting with a separate small ball (or long length) of yarn for each area of color and twisting yarns together on wrong side when changing color to avoid holes.
Note: The chart shows only the St st section of the blanket; the garter stitch borders are not included on the chart.

TO MAKE BLANKET
With size 6 (4mm) needles and MC, cast on 130 sts.
Work 10 rows in garter st (knit every row). Beg St st patt with garter st borders for center of cover as follows:
Next row (RS) Knit.
Next row K10, p110, k10.
Rep last 2 rows 18 times more, ending with a WS row.
Set position of chart patt (see pages 138–139) on next 2 rows as follows:
Next row (RS) K10; k next 110 sts foll chart row 1; k10.
Next row K10; p next 110 sts foll chart row 2; k10.
Cont foll chart as set and working 10-st garter st borders until all 162 rows of chart have been completed, ending with a WS row.
Then turn chart upside down and cont in patt by working all 162 rows in opposite direction—a total of 324 chart rows in total, ending with a WS row.
Using MC only for remainder of cover, work 38 rows in St st with 10-st garter st borders.
Work 10 rows in garter st.
Bind off knitwise.

TO FINISH
Block and press cover lightly on wrong side, following instructions on yarn label and avoiding garter st borders.

ROSETTE

If you or your pet are feeling unrewarded in the
gymkhana of life, why not knit your own rosette?
You can leave it plain or embroider whatever you
like in the center: 1st Prize, Runner-up, Best in Show.
The choice is up to you, but there's not much room,
so make it short.

R O S E T T E

LEVEL
Easy

SIZE
The finished rosette with pleated border measures approximately 4¾in/12cm in diameter and the tails measure approximately 5in/12.5cm and 6in/15.5cm long.

MATERIALS
1 x 1¾oz/50g ball of Rowan *Pure Wool DK* in main color **MC**, for rosette
Small amount of Rowan *Pure Wool DK* in a contrasting color **A**, for edging
Pair of size 6 (4mm) knitting needles
Small piece of cardboard, to stiffen rosette center
Safety pin

GAUGE
22 sts and 30 rows to 4in/10cm measured over St st using size 6 (4mm) needles.

ABBREVIATIONS
See page 17.

ROSETTE CENTER
With size 6 (4mm) needles and MC, cast on 10 sts.
Beg with a k row, work 2 rows in St st, ending with a p row.
Cont in St st throughout, inc 1 st at each end of next row and then at each end of 3 foll alt rows, ending with a k row. *(18 sts.)*
Work even in St st for 10 rows, ending with a k row.
Dec 1 st at each end of next row and then at each end of 3 foll alt rows, ending with a p row. *(10 sts.)*
Work even for 2 rows. Bind off.

PLEAT STRIP
With size 6 (4mm) needles and MC, cast on 120 sts.

For pleat with plain edging only
Beg with a k row, work 8 rows in St st, ending with a p (WS) row.

For pleat with a seeded edging only
Beg with a k row, work 7 rows in St st, ending with a k (RS) row.

For both versions
Break off MC and change to A.
Knit 1 row.
Bind off knitwise.

SHORT TAIL
With size 6 (4mm) needles and MC, cast on 8 sts. Work in garter st (knit every row) until tail measures 4in/10cm from cast-on edge.
**Divide tail
Before beg next row to divide tail, mark this side of work as RS, using a colored thread.

Next row (RS) K4, then turn, leaving rem sts on a st holder.
Working on these 4 sts only, cont as follows:
Next row (WS) K2tog, k2. *(3 sts.)*
Knit 1 row.
Next row K2tog, k1. *(2 sts.)*
Knit 1 row.
Next row K2tog, then break off MC, thread tail end through rem st, and pull tight to fasten off.
With RS facing, rejoin MC to 4 sts on st holder and k to end.
Next row (WS) K2, k2tog. *(3 sts.)*
Knit 1 row
Next row K1, k2tog. *(2 sts.)*
Knit 1 row.
Next row K2tog, then break off MC, thread tail end through rem st, and pull tight to fasten off.

LONG TAIL
With size 6 (4mm) needles and MC, cast on 8 sts.
Work in garter st (knit every row) until tail measures 6in/15cm from cast-on edge.
Complete as for short tail from **.

TO FINISH
Do not press.
Cut a circle of cardboard 2⅜in/6cm in diameter. Place cardboard circle on wrong side of knitted rosette center. Then using a blunt-ended yarn needle and a strand of MC, weave yarn in and out around edge of rosette center; pull tight to gather edge and enclose cardboard inside knitting, and fasten off. Using MC, sew safety pin to back of rosette center (over top of gathered edge).

Pleated border
Fold pleat strip into approximately 4-stitch pleats along cast-on edge (so that it will fit around rosette center), and sew pleats in place using MC. Using mattress stitch, sew ends of pleated strip together to form a ring. Sew pleated ring to back of rosette center, close to edge. Sew cast-on ends of tails (one on top of the other and with short tail to front) to wrong side of lower edge of rosette center.

ECO-DOG COATS

These are to inspire you to transform your favorite old sweater into a beautiful and completely individual coat for your dog. If, however, you want to keep your beloved old sweater for yourself, charity shops and rummage sales are a rich source of secondhand knitwear. These are ideas that you can elaborate on in your own unique way.

TWINSET AND PEARLS
DOG COAT

LEVEL
Easy

SIZE
The coat is made to fit your dog. It fits around the dog's body, buttons along the dog's belly, and has two legs for the dog's front legs.

MATERIALS
One old roundneck wool cardigan, and matching sewing thread
Small amount of black double-knitting-weight wool yarn
Disappearing fabric marker, to mark seams
20 large fake pearls with large holes (holes large enough for a blunt-ended tapestry needle and yarn to pass through)

CHOOSE AND FELT THE OLD CARDIGAN
For this design, we used a traditional long-sleeved wool stockinette stitch cardigan, with a grosgrain ribbon backing along the button and buttonhole bands.
A shrunken sweater or one with holes is ideal and it must be made of pure wool because it needs to be felted in a washing machine. Felting the sweater makes it easier to work with; you can cut straight into it without fear of fraying edges or running stitches.
Wash the cardigan with some detergent on a noncolorfast wash at 105°F/40°C. It will come out much smaller and will have a slight cardboard feel. Once dry, it will be more pliable.

TO MAKE THE COAT
Measure your dog as explained on page 10 to make sure the felted cardigan is big enough to be cut down to fit your dog.

(Fig 1) Then cut the sleeves off the old felted cardigan in a straight line from the underarm, and perpendicular to the sleeve seam, so that the sleeve forms a cap. Cut the ribbed cuffs off the bottom of the sleeves, including about ³/₈in/1cm of stockinette stitch above them.

Customizing to fit your dog
Catch your dog and slip the cardigan on him/her.
(Fig 2) Carefully pin a dart from the neck down the shoulder and onto the cap sleeve to reduce the width of the armhole—you may need to remove up to 1¹/₂in/3.5cm of knitted fabric. Then pin along the dog's back, taking up most of the excess knitted fabric.
Use a disappearing fabric marker to mark along the seam lines and remove the pins. Take the cardigan off the dog, turn it inside out, and pin along the marked lines at the shoulders and along the back. Baste the seams and remove the pins.

Sewing seams
Using a sewing machine (or hand sewing), stitch along these basted lines. Try the coat on your dog again and make any adjustments. Once satisfied, remove the basting, trim the seams, and turn the cardigan right side out. Overlock or zigzag stitch along the edges of the sleeves. Slip the stockinette stitch top of the cuff inside the end of the sleeve and sew the cuff to the sleeve, using a blunt-ended tapestry needle, black wool yarn, and decorative running stitches. Trim off the excess knitted fabric at the top of the cuff inside the coat.

TO APPLY FINISHING TOUCHES
Using a blunt-ended tapestry needle, black wool yarn, and running stitches, start at the button band and sew the pearls to the neck along the base of the neck ribbing. For a decorative effect, make one running stitch in between each pearl. Press and dress.

LEVEL
Easy

SIZE
The coat is made to fit your dog.
It fits around the dog's body, opens along the dog's belly, has two legs for the dog's front legs, buttons at the front of the dog, and is held in place by a belt.

MATERIALS
One old V-neck wool pullover
Piece of an old sweater in a contrasting color and matching sewing thread, for appliqué
Small amount of black double-knitting-weight wool yarn, for edging
2 buttons

CHOOSE AND PREPARE THE OLD PULLOVER
The pullover used for this design was a long-sleeved wool stockinette stitch V-neck with fine stripes. The belt was cut from one of the sleeves.
Felt the pullover (and a piece of an old sweater in a contrasting color for the appliqué), as explained on page 93 before beginning the coat.

TO MAKE THE COAT
Measure your dog as explained on page 10 to make sure the old felted pullover is big enough to be cut down to fit your dog. Then cut the sleeves off the old felted pullover in a straight line from the underarm, and perpendicular to the sleeve seam, so that the sleeve forms a cap (see page 93). Save the sleeves to make the belt.
Cut in a straight line from the point of the V-neck shaping down the center front.

Customizing to fit your dog
Slip the sweater on your dog, with his/her front legs in the sleeves and the newly cut front opening hanging under the dog's body. Depending on the size of the sweater and your dog, you will need to trim off some excess fabric along the front edges of the sweater. Carefully pin a dart from the neck down the shoulder and onto the cap sleeve to reduce the width of the armhole. You may also need to take out excess fabric down the center back. If so, pin along here as well.
Use a disappearing fabric marker to mark along the seam lines and remove the pins. Take the sweater off the dog, turn it inside out, and pin along the marked seam/dart lines. Baste the seams and remove the pins.

Sewing seams
Using a sewing machine (or hand sewing), stitch along these basted lines.
Try the coat on your dog again and make any adjustments. Once satisfied, remove the basting, trim the seams, and turn the coat right side out.

To prepare the belt
Measure around the dog's chest. Add an extra 2in/5cm to this measurement for the overlap at the fastening.
Cut a 2in/5cm wide strip for the belt from one of the sleeves of the felted pullover, trying to incorporate the cuff ribbing at one end of the belt. If you want ribbing at each end of the belt, cut half of the belt from each sleeve and sew the strips together at the center of the belt.

TO APPLY FINISHING TOUCHES
Cut a 1/2in/12mm slit for the buttonhole on one of the right front just below the pullover neck ribbing and 1/2in/12mm in from the front edge. Test the size of the buttonhole slit with the button and increase the length if necessary. Then, using a blunt-ended tapestry needle and black yarn, blanket stitch around the buttonhole.
Sew a button to the other side of the front opening.
Work a blanket stitch edging along the front edges of the coat, and then around the ends of the sleeves.

Appliqué
Enlarge a dog silhouette (see page 141 for a choice of templates) by 300–400% using a photocopier. Cut out the shape from the photocopy, pin it to the contrasting piece of felted knitting and cut out the appliqué.
Pin the appliqué to the back of the dog coat, either along the side or across the back. Then using a matching thread, machine zigzag stitch the appliqué in place around the edge. (Alternatively, stitch the appliqué in place by hand with running stitches, using a blunt-ended tapestry needles and a contrasting yarn.)

Belt fastening
For the belt fastening, make a buttonhole as before, 1in/2.5cm from one end of the belt, and sew a button to the other end. Press and dress.

JEWELED **DOG** COAT

LEVEL
Easy

SIZE
The coat is made to fit your dog. It fits across the dog's back, hangs down the dog's sides, buttons at the front of the dog, and is held in place by a belt.

MATERIALS
One old roundneck wool pullover
Remnant of cotton fabric or calico, or a sheet of newspaper, for "toile" pieces
Small amount of double-knitting-weight wool yarn in a contrasting color, for edging
Assortment of sew-on jewels
2 buttons

CHOOSE AND PREPARE THE OLD PULLOVER
The sweater used for this design was a simple roundneck, long-sleeved, stockinette stitch wool pullover. We used the back and front for the body of the coat and one sleeve for the belt.
Felt the sweater as explained on page 93 before beginning the coat.

TO MAKE THE "TOILE"
(Fig 1) This coat needs a pattern piece, or "toile," as a guide to cutting the pieces from the old felted pullover.
Measure your dog as explained on page 10.
Using the measurements you have taken from you dog as your guide, draw the shape of half of the coat on a piece of old material or calico—or if nothing else is available, a sheet of newspaper. The seam runs down the center of the dog's back, so halve the dog's neck and shoulder measurements and allow 1/4in/6mm extra for the center back seam allowance.
Draw a concave curve from the center back at the neck edge to the front edge of the coat, for the neck opening and the section that wraps around the front of the dog. (The two front extensions should

overlap about 1 1/4in/3cm at the front of the dog.)
Draw a 2in/5cm wide strip for the belt, long enough to fit around the dog's chest and overlap about 1 1/4in/3cm.
Cut out the "toile" pieces and try them on the dog, then make any necessary adjustments.

TO MAKE THE COAT
Cut the sleeves off the old felted pullover at the armholes, lay out the sweater flat, and place the coat "toile" on top. It is a good idea to try to incorporate the cuff ribbing either at the front edge of the dog's coat or at the tail-end edge of the coat, or both. Cutting around the "toile," cut out two pieces from the pullover for the coat.
Using the belt "toile," cut the belt from one sleeve of the pullover, again trying to incorporate the cuff ribbing at one end of the belt.

Sewing seam
Pin the two sides of the coat together along the center back, with the wrong sides together. With a contrasting yarn and a blunt-ended tapestry needle, sew the seam using blanket stitches 1/4in/6mm long. Try the coat on your dog again and make any final adjustments.

TO APPLY FINISHING TOUCHES
Cut a 1/2in/12mm slit for the buttonhole on one of the front extensions of the coat, 1in/2.5cm down from the neck edge and 1/2in/12mm in from the front edge. Test the size of the buttonhole slit with the button and increase the length if necessary. Then, using the contrasting yarn, blanket stitch around the buttonhole. Sew a button to the other side of the front opening.
Work a blanket stitch edging all around the outer edge of the coat, and then around the belt.
For the belt fastening, make a buttonhole as before, 1/2in/12mm from one end of the belt. Sew a button to the other end. Decorate the belt with sew-on jewels (available from craft stores).
Press and dress.

POMPOMS

Pompoms are very easy to make, and you probably know how to already. But in case you have forgotten, here are some pompoms to entertain your cat, dog, rat, ferret, snake—everyone enjoys a pompom. Ours are made from wool and a recycled plastic bag, but you can use string, raffia, ribbon, spaghetti, or anything you like really. Hours of fun for you and your pet.

POMPOMS

LEVEL
Easy

SIZE
The finished pompoms measure approximately 3in/7.5cm in diameter.
Note: To alter the size of the pompoms, cut smaller or larger cardboard circles.

MATERIALS
Wool pompom
Assorted colors of double-knitting-weight yarn
Plastic pompom
One clear or colored plastic bag, to make "yarn"
Both pompoms
Cardboard—a cereal box is ideal

WOOL POMPOM

CARDBOARD POMPOM TEMPLATES (MAKE 2)
Using a compass or drawing around the base of a mug, draw a circle about 3in/7.5cm in diameter on the cardboard (the size of the circle will be the size of finished pompom). Draw a 1in/2.5cm circle in the center of the first circle. Cut out the larger circle, then cut out the small circle at the center.
Make a second cardboard circle exactly the same.

TO MAKE POMPOM
Hold the two cardboard circles together and wind the yarn around the ring as evenly as possible until the hole is almost closed up with yarn (it is quicker to wind several strands at once). Then thread yarn onto a needle and continue to wind until the hole is closed up.
Cut the yarn around the edge of the circles, sliding a point of the scissors along in between the two pieces of cardboard. Ease the cardboard templates slightly apart and wrap a long length of doubled yarn between the templates and around the center of the pompom. Tie the pompom together tightly at the center, leaving two long tail ends of yarn hanging.
Then pull, or cut, the cardboard away from the pompom.

Fluff up the pompom and trim into shape if necessary. For a hanging cord, twist the two long ends of yarn together and knot.

PLASTIC POMPOM

TO PREPARE PLASTIC "YARN"
Prepare the plastic "yarn" as for the Water Lily on page 52.

TO MAKE POMPOM
Make the cardboard templates and the pompom as for the wool pompom, but be careful not to tear the plastic "yarn" and use ordinary yarn to tie the pompom at the center.

PUPPY PAPOOSE

This is a truly indispensable accessory for the
pet lover. If you have a small puppy or tiny dog,
you will inevitably spend a lot of the time carrying
it around. The solution is a soft, comfortable cradle
worn close to you. It will keep your puppy feeling
warm and secure.

PUPPY PAPOOSE

LEVEL
Intermediate

SIZES
Small—for a young puppy
The finished small size measures approximately 14in/36cm across
the widest part and 15in/38.5cm long.
Large—for an older puppy or a small dog
The finished large size measures approximately 16in/41cm across
the widest part and 17³/₄in/45cm long.

MATERIALS
3 x 1³/₄oz/50g balls of Rowan *Kid Classic* in main color **MC**
1 x 1³/₄oz/50g ball of Rowan *Kid Classic* in first contrasting color **A**,
for roses
1 x 1³/₄oz/50g ball of Rowan *Kid Classic* in second contrasting color **B**,
for leaves and stems
Pair of size 6 (4mm) knitting needles
Pair of size 5 (3.75mm) knitting needles
2¹/₄yd/2m of 2in/5cm satin ribbon, for backing the straps
18in/50cm of mattress ticking (or other strong, tightly woven fabric),
for lining the papoose
Matching sewing thread, for sewing on ribbon and making lining

GAUGE
24 sts and 30 rows to 4in/10cm over St st using size 6 (4mm) needles.
(**Note:** This needle size is smaller than the size recommended on the yarn label,
as it needs to be knitted tightly to help support the weight of the dog.)

ABBREVIATIONS
See page 17.

CHART NOTE
The chart is worked in St st. When working from the chart, read odd-numbered rows (k rows) from right to left, and even-numbered rows (p rows) from left to right. When working the chart pattern, use the intarsia method (see page 14), knitting with a separate small ball (or long length) of yarn for each area of color and twisting yarns together on wrong side when changing color to avoid holes.
Note: The chart shows only the St st section of the papoose; the seed stitch borders are not included on the chart.

TO MAKE PAPOOSE
With size 6 (4mm) needles and MC, cast on 13 sts.
Knit 1 row.
Next row [K1, p1, k1] all into each st to end (to inc twice into each st). *(39 sts.)*
Beg St st patt with seed st borders as follows:
Next row (RS) K1, [p1, k1] twice for seed st border; k into front and back of next st, k to last 6 sts, k into front and back of next st; [k1, p1] twice, k1 for seed st border.
Next row K1, [p1, k1] twice for seed st border; p into front and back of next st, p to last 6 sts, p into front and back of next st; [k1, p1] twice, k1 for seed st border.
Rep last 2 rows twice more. *(51 sts.)*
Set position of chart patt (see page 137) on next 2 rows (chart rows 7 and 8) as follows:
Next row (RS) Using MC seed st 5 sts; using MC k into front and back of next st,

k29MC, k1A, k9MC, using MC k into front and back of next st; using MC seed st 5 sts.

Next row Using MC seed st 5 sts; using MC p into front and back of next st, p9MC, p1A, p31MC, using MC p into front and back of next st; using MC seed st 5 sts.

Cont foll chart as set and working 5-st seed st borders in MC throughout **and at the same time** inc 1 st at each end (inside seed st borders) of next 6 (10) rows, ending with a WS row. *(67 (75) sts.)* Work 1 row without shaping.

Inc 1 st at each end of next row and then at each end of every foll alt row 9 (11) times, ending with a RS row. *(87 (99) sts.)* Omitting incomplete motifs on smaller size throughout, work even until chart row 78 (90) has been completed, ending with a WS row.

Dec 1 st at each end of next row and then at each end of every foll alt row 10 (12) times, ending with a RS row. *(65 (73) sts.)* Dec 1 st at each end of next 13 (17) rows (cont with MC only after last motif has been completed), ending with a WS row. *(39 sts.)*

Knit 1 row.

Next row (WS) [K3tog] 13 times. *(13 sts.)* Leave sts on a spare needle.

STRAPS (WORK 2)

Work a strap at each end of papoose as follows:

Strap 1

With RS facing and using size 5 (3.75mm) needles and MC, work seed st across 13 sts on spare needle as follows:

1st row (RS) *K1, p1; rep from * to last st, k1.

Rep last row until seed st strap measures 20in/51.5cm.

Shape top of strap

Keeping seed st correct as set, dec 1 st at beg of next row and than at same edge of every row 11 times in all. *(2 sts.)*

Next row K2tog, break off MC, thread tail end through rem st, and pull to fasten off.

Strap 2

For second strap, with RS facing and using size 5 (3.75mm) needles and MC, pick up and knit 13 sts along cast-on edge of papoose.

Work in seed st as for first strap until strap measures 26in/66.5cm.

Keeping seed st correct as set, dec 1 st at beg of next row and than at same edge of every row 11 times in all. *(2 sts.)*

Next row K2tog, break off MC, thread tail end through rem st, and pull to fasten off.

TO FINISH

Press lightly on wrong side, following instructions on yarn label.

Backing on straps

Cut a piece of ribbon to line each strap, allowing extra at ends for hems. Fold under ends of each length of ribbon, and pin and sew to wrong side of straps, using a sewing machine or handsewing with slip stitches. This ribbon backing will hold straps firm and prevent them from stretching.

Press straps lightly again.

Lining on papoose

Following measurements given in the diagrams below, draw an outline of the lining for the small **(Fig 1)** or large size

(Fig 2) on a piece of newspaper. Then add an extra 1/2in/1.5cm all around the edge for a hem allowance. Fold newspaper lining pattern in half and cut it out around the outline.

Fold lining fabric in half and pin folded pattern piece on top of it. Then cut the fabric out around paper pattern.

Using a sewing machine, work long, loose gathering stitches along top of lining about 3/8in/12mm from edge, starting at bottom of curve where dotted line crosses outline on one side (3 1/2in/9cm down from top) and ending at same place on other side of top. Work gathering stitches along bottom of lining in same way.

Pull gathering stitches at top of lining to gather fabric so that it fits across top of knitted papoose piece. Fold 1/2in/1.5cm to wrong side along this gathered edge so that gathering stitches are on wrong side of lining, pin, and baste. Stitch this hem in place and remove basting.

Gather and stitch bottom edge of lining in same way.

Fold 1/2in/1.5cm to wrong side along side edges of lining, press, and stitch in place.

Pin gathered edges of lining to top and bottom ends of papoose and sew in place. Leave long, straight side edges of lining loose.

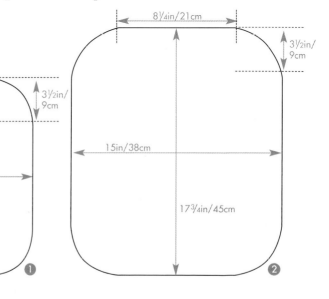

HAMSTER HOUSE

A collaborative housing project for you and your rodent. No more living in a cardboard box or shapeless ball of sawdust-covered fluff. In no time at all you can knit your hamster a magnificent new house. And if your hamster feels inclined, he can then recycle it into a bed of his own design.

HAMSTER HOUSE

LEVEL
Easy

SIZE
The finished hamster house measures approximately $11\frac{3}{4}$in/29.5cm in circumference by $4\frac{1}{2}$in/11.5cm tall, not including tassel at top.

MATERIALS
1 x $3\frac{1}{2}$oz/100g ball of Rowan *Scottish Tweed Aran* in main color **MC**, for house
Small amount of a fine-weight yarn in a contrasting color **A**, for tassel
Pair of size 5 (3.75mm) knitting needles
Crochet hook, for attaching tassel

GAUGE
19 sts and 27 rows to 4in/10cm measured over St st using size 5 (3.75mm) needles.
Note: The house is knitted tighter than suggested on the yarn label so that it is firm enough to stand up.

ABBREVIATIONS
See page 17.

TO MAKE HOUSE
With size 5 (3.75mm) needles and MC, cast on 56 sts.
Work 6 rows in garter stitch (knit every row).
Mark each end of last row with a colored thread.
Cont in garter st, bind off 3 sts at beg of each of next 2 rows, then 2 sts at beg of 2 foll rows. (46 sts.)
Work even in garter st for 6 rows.
Cont in garter st, cast on 2 sts at beg of each of next 2 rows, then 3 sts at beg of 2 foll rows. (56 sts.)
Mark each end of last row with a colored thread.
Work even in garter st for 8 rows.

Shape top
Change to St st and shape top of house as follows:
Next row (RS) [K2tog, k5] 8 times. *(48 sts.)*
Purl 1 row.
Next row [K2tog, k4] 8 times. *(40 sts.)*
Purl 1 row.
Next row [K2tog, k3] 8 times. *(32 sts.)*
Purl 1 row.
Next row [K2tog, k2] 8 times. *(24 sts.)*
Purl 1 row.
Next row [K2tog, k1] 8 times. *(16 sts.)*
Purl 1 row.
Next row [K2tog] 8 times. *(8 sts.)*
Purl 1 row.
Next row [K2tog] 4 times. *(4 sts.)*
Purl 1 row.
Next row [K2tog] twice. *(2 sts.)*
Next row P2tog, then break off MC, thread tail end through rem st, and pull tight to fasten off.

TO FINISH
Do not press.
Join house at center front to form it into a circle as follows:
With right sides together, sew together side edges of knitting between cast-on edge and first set of markers; then sew together side edges of knitting between second set of markers and top point of house. Turn right side out.

Tassel
Cut five strands of A, each 4in/10cm long. Holding strands together, fold them in half and use a crochet hook to pull loop at folded end of strands through top of house. Still using hook, pull ends of strands through loop, then pull ends tight to secure tassel in place.
Trim ends of tassel to desired length.

WIRE **BIRD** FEEDER

Wild birds are hardly pets, we know, but they are
crucial members of the animal world, so it is worth
the effort to knit this bird feeder. For the enterprising,
this is an opportunity to increase your knitting skills.
A treat for you and the wild birds in your garden.

WIRE **BIRD** FEEDER

LEVEL
Difficult until you have mastered knitting with wire, then intermediate

SIZE
The finished bird feeder measures approximately 3¼in/8.5cm in diameter by 10in/25.5cm long.

MATERIALS
64yd/58m of 0.5mm wire **A** in silver, for bird feeder
21yd/19m of 0.5mm wire **B** in brass, for bird
1yd/1m of 1mm wire **C** in silver, for bird feeder handle
Pair of size 5 (3.75mm) knitting needles
Pair of size 3 (3mm) knitting needles
Blunt-ended tapestry needle, for sewing seams with wire
Tough scissors or pliers, for cutting and twisting wire
2 lengths of wooden doweling, 9mm in diameter and 6in/15cm long,
OR 2 sticks from garden

GAUGE
Approximately 16 sts and 20 rows to 4in/10cm measured over garter st using size 5 (3.75mm) needles and wire A.

ABBREVIATIONS
See page 17.

TIPS FOR KNITTING WITH WIRE
Knitting with wire can be a little harsh on your hands, but persevere as it is very rewarding. If you have never knit with wire before, here are a few hints that will make it easier:
• Do not use your best needles—we use old aluminum ones.
• Because wire has no stretch, all stitches need to be worked loosely so that you can easily slip the needle into the loops.
• Cast on using the simplest method—the "backward through loop" cast-on (also called the "thumb" cast-on). To cast on with this method, hold the wire in your right hand and wrap it over your left thumb

clockwise and around so it crosses over itself. Next, insert the knitting needle into the loop from below and slip the loop off your thumb; make sure the new cast-on loop now on the right needle is loose. Wrap the wire around your thumb again, but this time without making a crossed loop; then insert the needle into the loop from below and slip the loop onto the needle. Continue adding loops in this way.
• Garter stitch is the best stitch to use with wire because of the effect achieved. It has more bounce and is easy to work.
• Wire has almost no weight and the stitches don't "drop" naturally as you knit, so after every two rows pull on the knitting

to stretch it downward.
• To increase in the middle of a row, make a yarn-over (yo). To increase at the beginning or end of a row, cast on a stitch.
• Always bind off knitwise.

MAIN SECTION OF BIRD FEEDER
With size 5 (3.75mm) needles and wire A, cast on 40 sts, using "backward loop" cast-on (see left)
Work 11 rows in garter st (knit every row).
Working in garter st throughout, cont as follows:
Next row K5, k2tog, k18, k2tog, k13.
Next row K14, yo, k18, yo, k6.

Work even for 17 rows.
Next row K13, k2tog, k18, k2tog, k5.
Next row K6, yo, k18, yo, k14.
Work even for 19 rows (a total of 51 rows worked from cast-on edge).
Bind off loosely knitwise.

CIRCULAR BASE OF BIRD FEEDER
With size 5 (3.75mm) needles and wire A, cast on 6 sts.
Work 2 rows in garter st.
Working in garter st throughout, cont as follows:
Inc 1 st at each end of next row and then at each end of 4 foll alt rows. *(16 sts.)*
Work even for 6 rows.
Dec 1 st at each end of next row and then at each end of 4 foll alt rows. *(6 sts.)*
Work even for 2 rows.
Bind off loosely knitwise.

CIRCULAR LID OF BIRD FEEDER
Work exactly as for circular base of bird feeder.

RIM FOR LID
With size 5 (3.75mm) needles and wire A, cast on 52 sts.
Work 3 rows in garter st.
Bind off knitwise.

BIRD
With size 3 (3mm) needles and wire B, cast on 8 sts.
Work bird in garter st as follows:
1st–4th rows Knit.
5th row Cast on 1 st, knit to end, cast on 1 st. *(10 sts.)*
6th–8th rows Knit.
9th row Cast on 1 st, k2, yo, k2, [yo] twice, k2, yo, k2, cast on 1 st. *(16 sts.)*
10th row Knit.
11th row Cast on 1 st, k4, [yo, k2] 3 times, yo, k4, cast on 1 st. *(22 sts.)*
12th row Knit.
13th row Cast on 1 st, k5, yo, k10, yo, k5, cast on 1 st. *(26 sts.)*
14th row Knit.
15th row Cast on 1 st, k6, yo, k12, yo, k6, cast on 1 st. *(30 sts.)*
16th row Knit.
17th row Cast on 1 st, k28, cast on 1 st. *(32 sts.)*
18th–20th rows Knit.
21st row K2tog, k6, k2tog, k12, k2tog, k6, k2tog. *(28 sts.)*
22nd row Knit.
23rd row K2tog, k5, k2tog, k10, k2tog, k5, k2tog. *(24 sts.)*
24th row Knit.
25th row K2tog, k4, k2tog, k8, k2tog, k4, k2tog. *(20 sts.)*
26th row [K2tog, k7] twice, k2tog. *(17 sts.)*
27th row K2tog, k5, k2tog, k6, k2tog. *(14 sts.)*
28th–30th rows Knit.
31st row K4, yo, k6, yo, k4. *(16 sts.)*
32nd row Knit.
33rd row K4, yo, k8, yo, k4. *(18 sts.)*
34th row K4, yo, k10, yo, k4. *(20 sts.)*
35th row K2tog, k3, k2tog, k6, k2tog, k3, k2tog. *(16 sts.)*
36th row K2tog, k2, k2tog, k4, k2tog, k2, k2tog. *(12 sts.)*
37th row [K2tog] twice, k4, [k2tog] twice. *(8 sts.)*
38th row [K2tog] 4 times. *(4 sts.)*
39th row K2tog twice, cut wire (leaving a long length for sewing up bird), slip end of wire through rem 2 sts, pull gently to close loop, and pinch wire together to make a point for beak.

TO FINISH
Use a blunt-ended tapestry needle and matching wire to sew all seams.

Bird feeder
Using slip stitch, sew together two side edges of main section of bird feeder to make a tube, and sew circular base to bottom of feeder. Then cut a 12in/30.5cm length of wire A and secure it to bottom of main section of feeder opposite seam running up tube; run this length of wire through knitting around base and twist ends together to reinforce shape at base.
Cut a 11in/28cm length of wire C, weave it through top row of bird feeder to make a firm circle for lid to sit on; twist ends together to secure.
Cut a 12in/30.5cm length of wire C and loop it through seam of feeder 1/2in/12mm from bound-off edge and twist end to secure. Then curve it to make a handle, slip other end into feeder at same position on opposite side, and twist end to secure. Slip two lengths of doweling (or two sticks) through holes in feeder.

Bird feeder lid
Sew together cast-on and bound-off ends of rim to form a circle, and sew it to cicular lid with overcast stitch.

Bird's body
Curve bird to make correct shape (see photograph). Then starting at head, sew together two side edges using slip stitch (to form a seam running from tip of beak down center of bird's front and belly, and to tip if underside of tail). When you reach tail, flatten it out and sew across end of tail (cast-on edge), leaving a length of wire to attach tail to lid.

Bird's feet
Cut a length of wire B about 16in/40.5cm, long, fold it in half and twist it together. Slip twisted wire through belly of bird and make a V-shape at each end for feet.
Using spare wire from feet, attach bird's feet to lid, then attach tail to lid.
Fill feeder with nuts, put lid in place, hang outside, and wait for the flocks to flock.

KNITTED PETS

Cleaner, quieter, cheaper—these are just some of the
advantages of the knitted pet. Make your own tiny
fox terrier, better behaved that the real version and
almost as adorable. An obvious benefit of the knitted
ferret is that he has no teeth. Also, he won't object
to being dressed up. Ours comes with a scarf,
but see www.ferretworld.co.uk for further inspiration.
The guinea pig is very simple and comes smooth or
rough coated—just slip his coat on or off. You'll never
need to clean out his cage and he won't be eaten by
foxes. Unlike the live version, these tortoises are
extremely cheap and easy to knit, and if necessary,
you can remove the shell and wash them. You also
won't have the anxiety about tortoise rustlers.

FOX TERRIER

LEVEL
Intermediate

SIZE
The finished fox terrier measures approximately 12¹/₂in/32cm long with legs outstretched to front and back.

MATERIALS
1 x 1³/₄oz/50g ball of Rowan *Kid Classic* in main color **MC** (off-white/Feather 829), for dog's body and legs
1 x 1³/₄oz/50g ball of Jaeger *Matchmaker Merino DK* in **A** (camel brown/Syrup 789), for markings on dog and ears
1 x 1³/₄oz/50g ball of Jaeger *Matchmaker Merino 4-Ply* in **B** (light sea blue/Mineral 741), for dog's coat
Small amount of a fine-weight yarn in black, for embroidered nose and eyes
Pair of size 6 (4mm) knitting needles
Pair of size 3 (3.25mm) knitting needles
Toy filling
4 small white buttons, for securing legs to dog
Crochet hook, for attaching whiskers

GAUGE
22 sts and 30 rows to 4in/10cm measured over St st using size 6 (4mm) needles and MC. (**Note:** This needle size is smaller than the size recommended on the yarn label, but the fox terrier needs to be knitted tightly.)

ABBREVIATIONS
See page 17.

LEFT SIDE OF BODY
Each side of the dog's body is worked starting at the belly edge and working upward toward the dog's spine.
With size 6 (4mm) needles and MC, cast on 12 sts.
Beg with a k row, work 4 rows in St st, ending with a p row.

Shape belly
Cont in St st throughout and beg with a k row, cast on 6 sts at beg of next row. *(18 sts.)*
Work even for 3 rows, ending with a p row.

Cast on 4 sts at beg of next row. *(22 sts.)*
Work even for 5 rows, ending with a p row.
Cast on 8 sts at beg of next row. *(30 sts.)*
Work even for 6 rows, ending with a k row.

Work marking on dog's back
Using MC and A as required, work marking on dog's back as follows:
Next row (WS) P20MC, p10A.
Next row K11A, k19MC.
Next row P18MC, p12A.
Next row K13A, k17MC.
Break off A and cont with MC only.

Shape neck
Next row (WS) P14, then turn, leaving rem 16 sts on a spare needle.
Working on these 14 sts only, cont as follows:
Dec 1 st at beg of next row and then at beg of 2 foll alt rows, ending with a k row. *(11 sts.)*
Purl 1 row.
Slip these 11 sts onto a st holder.

Shape tail
With WS facing, rejoin A to 16 sts on spare needle, bind off 10 sts purlwise (along dog's spine) and p to end. *(6 sts.)*

Working on these 6 sts only, cont as follows:
Work even for 4 rows, ending with a p row.
Next row (RS) *K2tog, k to last st, k into front and back of last st. *(6 sts.)*
Purl 1 row.
Rep last 2 rows once more.
Work even for 2 rows.
Bind off.

RIGHT SIDE OF BODY
With size 6 (4mm) needles and MC, cast on 12 sts.
Beg with a k row, work 3 rows in St st, ending with a k row.

Shape belly
Cont in St st throughout and beg with a p row, cast on 6 sts at beg of next row. *(18 sts.)*
Work even for 3 rows, ending with a k row.
Cast on 4 sts at beg of next row. *(22 sts.)*
Work even for 5 rows, ending with a k row.
Cast on 8 sts at beg of next row. *(30 sts.)*
Work even for 10 rows, ending with a p row.

Shape neck
Next row (RS) K14, then turn, leaving rem 16 sts on a spare needle.
Working on these 14 sts only, cont as follows:
Dec 1 st at beg of next row and then at beg of 2 foll alt rows, ending with a p row. *(11 sts.)*
Slip these 11 sts onto a second st holder and do not break off yarn.

Shape tail
With RS facing, rejoin another ball of MC to 16 sts on spare needle, bind off 10 sts (along dog's spine) and k to end. *(6 sts.)*
Working on these 6 sts only, cont as follows:
Break off MC and change to A.
Work even for 4 rows, ending with a k row.
Next row (WS) *P2tog, p to last st,

p into front and back of last st. *(6 sts.)*
Purl 1 row.
Rep last 2 rows once more.
Work even for 2 rows.
Bind off.

RIGHT FRONT LEG
Each leg is worked starting at foot end of leg.
With size 6 (4mm) needles and MC, cast on 16 sts.
Beg with a k row, work 24 rows in St st, ending with a p row.
Work marking on leg
Using MC and A as required, work colored marking on leg as follows:
Next row (RS) K13MC, k3A.
Next row P4A, p12MC.
Next row K11MC, k5A.
Next row P6A, p10MC.
Cont in St st, working 1 st more into A on each row until 34 rows St st have been worked from cast-on edge.
Bind off.

LEFT FRONT LEG
With size 6 (4mm) needles and MC, cast on 16 sts.
Beg with a k row, work 34 rows in St st.
Bind off.

RIGHT BACK LEG
**With size 6 (4mm) needles and MC, cast on 16 sts.
Beg with a k row, work 10 rows in St st, ending with a p row.****

Shape leg
Cont in St st throughout and beg with a k row, inc 1 st at each end of next row and then at each end of every foll k row until there are 32 sts, ending with a k row.
Work even for 5 rows, ending with a p row.
Dec 1 st at each end of next 4 rows. *(24 sts.)*
Bind off.

LEFT BACK LEG
Work as for right back leg from ** to **.

Shape leg
Cont in St st throughout and beg with a k row, inc 1 st at each end of next row and at each end of every foll k row until there are 22 sts, ending with a k row.
Purl 1 row.
Work marking on leg
Using MC and A as required, work colored marking on leg as follows:
Next row (RS) Using MC k into front and back of first st, k11MC, k9A, using A k into front and back of last st. *(24 sts.)*
Next row P12A, p12MC.
Next row Using MC k into front and back of first st, k12MC, k10A, using A k into front and back of last st. *(26 sts.)*
Next row P15A, p11MC.
Next row Using MC k into front and back of first st, k9MC, k15A, using A k into front and back of last st. *(28 sts.)*
Next row P18A, p10MC.
Next row Using MC k into front and back of first st, k8MC, k18A, using A k into front and back of last st. *(30 sts.)*
Next row P20A, p10MC.
Next row Using MC k into front and back of first st, k8MC, k20A, using A k into front and back of last st. *(32 sts.)*
Next row P23A, p9MC.
Break off A and cont with MC only.
Work even for 4 rows, ending with a p row.
Dec 1 st at each end of next 4 rows. *(24 sts.)*
Bind off.

HEAD
With RS facing and using size 6 (4mm) needles and MC (use ball of MC still attached to neck sts on right side of body), k 11 sts from holder on right side of body, then k 11 sts from holder on left side of body. *(22 sts.)*
Purl 1 row.

Shape top of head
Next row (RS) K15, pick up loop below next st on left needle by inserting tip of right needle from back to front through loop (this prevents a hole forming when turning work), then turn, leaving rem

7 sts on left needle unworked.
Work head shaping on 8 sts only as follows:
Next row P2tog (first st is loop picked up at end of last row), p7, pick up loop below next st on left needle by inserting tip of right needle from back to front through loop, then turn, leaving rem 7 sts on left needle unworked.
Next row K2tog (first st is loop picked up at end of last row), k7, pick up loop below next st on left needle, turn.
Next row P2tog (first st is loop picked up at end of last row), p7, pick up loop below next st on left needle, turn.
Rep last 2 rows twice more.
Next row K2tog (first st is loop picked up at end of last row), k7, pick up loop below next st on left needle, turn.
Next row P2tog (first st is loop picked up at end of last row), k14.
Next row K22.

Shape muzzle flap
Bind off 7 sts at beg of next 2 rows, ending with k row. (8 sts.)
Beg with a p row, work even for 10 rows in St st, ending with a k row.
Next row (WS) K to end, to form ridge on RS for foldline at nose.
Beg with a k row, work 5 rows in St st.
Next row (WS) K to end, to form ridge on RS for foldline at mouth.
Beg with a k row, work 8 rows in St st.
Bind off.

CHEEKS (MAKE 2)
With size 6 (4mm) needles and MC, cast on 6 sts.
Beg with a k row, work 9 rows in St st.
Bind off.
Make second cheek in same way.

EARS (MAKE 2)
With size 6 (4mm) needles and A, cast on 6 sts.
Beg with a k row, work 3 rows in St st, ending with a k row.
Next row (WS) K to end, to form ridge on RS for ear foldline.
Beg with a k row, work 3 rows in St st, ending with a k row.
Next row (WS) P2tog, p2, p2tog. (4 sts.)
Knit 1 row.
Next row [P2 tog] twice. (2 sts.)
Knit 1 row.

Next row P2tog, break off MC, thread tail end through rem st, and pull to fasten off. Make second ear in same way.

TOP OF DOG'S COAT
With size 3 (3.25mm) needles and B, cast on 30 sts.
1st rib row (RS) *K2, p2; rep from * to last 2 sts, k2.
2nd rib row *P2, k2; rep from * to last 2 sts, p2.
Rep last 2 rows 4 times more, ending with a WS row (10 rows in k2, p2 rib worked from cast-on edge).

Shape coat
Cont in k2, p2 rib and taking increased sts into rib patt, inc 1 st at each end of next row and then at each end of every foll 4th row until there are 40 sts, ending with a RS row.
Work 6 rows in rib as set, ending with a RS row.

Shape neck
Next row (WS) [P2tog] 20 times. (20 sts.)
Next row [K2tog] 10 times. (10 sts.)
Break off B and leave these neck sts on a st holder.

UNDERSIDE OF DOG'S COAT
With size 3 (3.25mm) needles and B, cast on 24 sts.
1st rib row (RS) *K1, p1; rep from * to end.
Rep last row 27 times more, ending with a WS row.

Join to top of coat
Next row (RS) Work 24 sts in k1, p1 rib as set, then with RS facing, cont in k1, p1 rib across 10 sts on st holder on top of coat. (34 sts.)

Collar
Work 8 rows more in k1, p1 rib.
Bind off in rib.

TO FINISH
Press left and right sides of body and legs lightly on wrong side, following instructions on yarn label. Do not press muzzle flap, ears, or coat pieces.

Body
Sew cheeks to sides of muzzle flap,

bending muzzle flap around cheeks.
Sew two sides of body together along throat, chest, belly, tail, and spine, leaving an opening in chest for inserting toy filling. Insert toy filling and sew opening closed.

Legs
Fold each leg in half lengthwise and sew seam along cast-on edges and side edges, leaving bound-off end open.
Insert toy filling in each leg, leaving about 1/2in/1.5cm at top of leg unstuffed (to allow for securing top of leg to body with a button).
Sew seam at top of each leg (bound-off edge).
Sew each leg to body as shown, securing it by sewing through a button at center of top of leg and into body.

Ears
Sew cast-on edge of each ear to head, positioning so that St st side of ear is on top and ears flop forward at foldline ridge.

Eyes and nose
Using black yarn, work two French knots for eyes and satin stitch for nose, positioning nose on nose ridge.

Whiskers
Cut two 3in/7.5cm lengths of MC.
Holding lengths together, fold in half and use a crochet hook to pull looped end through a single loop on dog's head about 3/8in/1cm from nose and level with nose. Pull ends of yarn through loop and pull to tighten. Attach two more whisker tufts in same way close to first tuft, working away from nose.
Attach three more whisker tufts on other side of nose in same way. Trim whiskers to 3/8in/1cm from knots.

Coat
Sew underside of coat to top of coat along side edges, leaving an opening 1in/2.5cm long for legholes.
Dress your terrier.

FERRET

LEVEL
Intermediate

SIZE
The finished ferret measures approximately 14½in/37cm long from mouth to tip of tail.

MATERIALS
1 x 1¾oz/50g ball of Rowan *Pure Wool DK* or Jaeger *Matchmaker Merino DK* in main color **MC** (rust), for top side of ferret's body and head
1 x 1¾oz/50g ball of Rowan *Pure Wool DK* or Jaeger *Matchmaker Merino DK* in contrasting color **A** (dark brown), for tail, legs, and ears
1 x 1¾oz/50g ball of Rowan *Pure Wool DK* or Jaeger *Matchmaker Merino DK* in contrasting color **B** (off-white), for claws and underside of ferret's body and head
1 x 1¾oz/50g ball of Rowan *4-Ply Soft* or Jaeger *Matchmaker Merino 4-Ply* in contrasting color **C** (dusky lilac), for scarf
Small amount of double-knitting weight yarn in black, for embroidered nose
Pair of size 6 (4mm) knitting needles
Pair of size 3 (3.25mm) knitting needles
Toy filling
2 small black buttons, for eyes

GAUGE
22 sts and 30 rows to 4in/10cm measured over St st using size 6 (4mm) needles and MC.

ABBREVIATIONS
See page 17.

TAIL AND TOP OF BODY AND HEAD
This section is worked starting at the tail.

Shape tail
With size 6 (4mm) needles and A, cast on 1 st.
1st row K into front and back of st. *(2 sts.)*
2nd row P to end.
Cont in St st throughout and beg with a k row, inc 1 st at each end of next row and then at each end every alt row 5 times, ending with a k row. *(14 sts.)*
Purl 1 row.

Inc 1 st each end of next row and each end of every foll 4th row until there are 28 sts.
Cont in St st throughout, work until tail measures 15cm/6in from cast-on edge, ending with a p row.
Next row (RS) [K3tog] 9 times, k1. *(10 sts.)*

Begin body
Break off A and change to MC.
Inc 1 st at each end of next 2 rows. *(14 sts.)*
Purl 1 row.
**Next row (RS) K into front and back of first st, k2, k into front and back of next

st, k to last 4 sts, k into front and back of next st, k2, k into front and back of last st.
Purl 1 row.******
Rep from ** to ** 3 times more. *(30 sts.)*
Work even until work measures 3in/7cm from beginning of body, ending with a p row.

Shape humpback
Next row (RS) K26, pick up loop below next st on left needle by inserting tip of right needle from back to front through loop (this prevents a hole forming when turning work), then turn, leaving rem

4 sts on left needle unworked.
Work hump on 22 sts only as follows:
Next row P2tog (first st is loop picked up at end of last row), p21, pick up loop below next st on left needle by inserting tip of right needle from back to front through loop, then turn, leaving rem 4 sts on left needle unworked.
Next row K2tog (first st is loop picked up at end of last row), k21, pick up loop below next st on left needle, turn.
Next row P2tog (first st is loop picked up at end of last row), p21, pick up loop below next st on left needle, turn.
Rep last 2 rows once more.
Next row K2tog (first st is loop picked up at end of last row), k25.
Next row P30.
Work even for 6 rows, ending with a p row.

Shape neck
Dec 1 st at each end of next row. (28 sts.)
Work even for 3 rows, ending with a p row.
Dec 1 st at each end of next row. (26 sts.)
Purl 1 row.
Next row** K2tog, k2, k2tog, k to last 6 sts, k2tog, k2, k2tog. (22 sts.)
Work even for 3 rows, ending with a p row.
Rep from *** to *** once. (18 sts.)
Work even for 9 rows, ending with a p row.

Shape head
Next row (RS) K15, pick up loop below next st on left needle, then turn, leaving rem 3 sts on left needle unworked.
Work head shaping on 12 sts only as follows:
Next row P2tog (first st is loop picked up at end of last row), p11, pick up loop below next st on left needle, then turn, leaving rem 3 sts on left needle unworked.
Next row K2tog (first st is loop picked up at end of last row), k11, pick up loop below next st on left needle, turn.
Next row P2tog (first st is loop picked up at end of last row), p11, pick up loop below next st on left needle, turn.
Rep last 2 rows once more.
Next row K2tog (first st is loop picked up at end of last row), k14.
Next row P18.

Shape muzzle
Next row (RS) K6, then turn, leaving rem 12 sts unworked.
Working on these 6 sts only, cont as follows:
Purl 1 row.
Next row K2tog, k4. (5 sts.)
Purl 1 row.
Next row K2tog, k3. (4 sts.)
Purl 1 row.
Next row K2tog, k2. (3 sts.)
Purl 1 row.
Next row K2tog, k1. (2 sts.)
Next row P2tog, break off MC, and fasten off.
With RS facing, rejoin MC to rem 12 sts, k 6 center sts, then turn, leaving rem 6 sts unworked.
Working on these 6 center sts only, cont as follows:
Purl 1 row.
Next row K2tog, k2, k2tog. (4 sts.)
Next row P2tog, p2tog. (2 sts.)
Next row K2tog, break off MC, and fasten off.
With RS facing, rejoin MC to rem 6 sts and k to end.
Purl 1 row.
Next row K4, k2tog. (5 sts.)
Purl 1 row.
Next row K3, k2tog. (4 sts.)
Purl 1 row.
Next row K2, k2tog. (3 sts.)
Purl 1 row.
Next row K1, k2tog. (2 sts.)
Next row P2tog, break off MC, and fasten off.

UNDERSIDE OF BODY AND HEAD
This section is worked starting at the head.

Shape underside of mouth and neck
With size 6 (4mm) needles and B, cast on 2 sts.
1st row (RS) K into front and back of each st. (4 sts.)
Cont in St st throughout and beg with a p row, work even for 3 rows, ending with a p row.
Inc 1 st at each end of next row. (6 sts.)
Work even for 7 rows, ending with a p row.
Inc 1 st at each end of next row. (8 sts.)
Work even for 11 rows, ending with a p row.
Inc 1 st at each end of next row. (10 sts.)
Work even for 5 rows, ending with a p row.
Inc 1 st at each end of next row. (12 sts.)

Work even for 25 rows, ending with a p row.
Dec 1 st at each end of next row and then at each end of every alt row 3 times, ending with a k row. (4 sts.)
Purl 1 row.
Next row [K2tog] twice.
Purl 1 row.
Next row K2tog, break off B, and fasten off.

EARS (MAKE 2)
With size 6 (4mm) needles and A, cast on 7 sts.
Beg with a k row, work 3 rows in St st, ending with a k row.
Bind off knitwise.
Make second ear in same way.

FRONT LEGS (MAKE 2)
The front legs are worked starting at the top of the leg.

Shape leg
With size 6 (4mm) needles and A, cast on 20 sts.
Beg with a k row, work 6 rows in St st, ending with a p row.
****Next row (RS)** K2tog, k to last 2 sts, k2tog.
Purl 1 row.
Rep last 2 rows 3 times more. (12 sts.)

Shape heel
Next row (RS) K9, pick up loop below next st on left needle, then turn, leaving rem 3 sts on left needle unworked.
Work heel shaping on 6 sts only as follows:
Next row P2tog (first st is loop picked up at end of last row), p5, pick up loop below next st on left needle, then turn, leaving rem 3 sts on left needle unworked.
Next row K2tog (first st is loop picked up at end of last row), k5, pick up loop below next st on left needle, turn.
Next row P2tog (first st is loop picked up at end of last row), p5, pick up loop below next st on left needle, turn.
Rep last 2 rows once more.
Next row K2tog (first st is loop picked up at end of last row), k8.
Mark each end of last row with a piece of colored thread.

Shape foot
Next row P2tog, p8, p2tog. (10 sts.)
Next row K2tog, k6, k2tog. (8 sts.)

Next row P2tog, p4, p2tog. *(6 sts.)*
Next row K2tog, k2, k2tog. *(4 sts.)*
Next row [P2tog] twice. *(2 sts.)*
Next row K2tog, break off A, and fasten off.
Make second leg in same way.

BACK LEGS (MAKE 2)
The back legs are worked starting at the top of the leg.

Shape leg
With size 6 (4mm) needles and A, cast on 20 sts.
Beg with a k row, work 4 rows in St st, ending with a p row.
Complete as for front legs from ****.
Make second leg in same way.

SCARF
With size 3 (3.25mm) needles and C, cast on 8 sts.
Work in garter st (knit every row) until the scarf measures 11in/28cm from the cast-on edge. Bind off knitwise.

TO FINISH
Do not press pieces.
Muzzle
Sew the two muzzle seams to join sides of muzzle to center section, easing in side sections.

Body
Sew underside of body and head to top of body and head, leaving an opening in seam for inserting toy filling.
Insert toy filling in body and sew opening closed.

Tail
Sew side edges of tail together. (Do not insert toy filling in tail.)

Ears
Sew cast-on edge of ears to top of head as shown (above head shaping turning rows), gathering edge slightly and positioning so that ears curl downward and rev St st side is on top.

Legs
Sew together side edges of one front leg, stitching from cast-on edge to markers so that foot is left open.
Sew seams on three remaining legs in same way.
Insert toy filling in each leg, then pinch together top of leg (cast-on edge) and sew so that leg seam is at one end of top seam.
Sew short back legs to seam lines between top and underside of ferret (one on each side), about 1/2in/1.5cm from tail. Sew long front legs to same seam line and about 2¾in/7cm in front of back legs.
Using B, embroider three short stitches around front of each foot for claws as shown in photograph.

Eyes and nose
Sew on buttons for eyes.
Embroider nose with black yarn.
Tie scarf around neck.

GUINEA PIG

LEVEL
Easy

SIZE
The finished guinea pig measures approximately 8in/20.5cm long.

MATERIALS
1 x 1³/₄oz/50g ball of Rowan *Kid Classic* in main color **MC** (charcoal/Smoke 831), for guinea pig
Small amount of Rowan *Kid Classic* in contrasting color **A** (pale pink/Sherbet Dip 850), for embroidered feet, mouth, and nose
1 x ⁷/₈oz/25g ball of Rowan *Kidsilk Haze* in contrasting color **B** (light brown), for coat
Pair of size 6 (4mm) knitting needles
Pair of size 8 (5mm) knitting needles
Toy filling
2 small buttons, for eyes

GAUGE
Body: 22 sts and 30 rows to 4in/10cm measured over St st using size 6 (4mm) needles and MC.
(**Note:** This needle size is smaller than recommended on the yarn label, but the guinea pig must be knitted tightly.)
Coat: 18 sts and 27 rows to 4in/10cm measured over loopy stitch using size 8 (5mm) needles and B.

ABBREVIATIONS
See page 17.

TOP OF BODY
With size 6 (4mm) needles and MC, cast on 12 sts (head end of toy).
Beg with a k row, work in St st, inc 1 st at each end of first 4 rows, ending with a p row. *(20 sts.)*
Cont in St st throughout and beg with a k row, work even for 6 rows, ending with a p row.
Inc 1 st at each end of next row. *(22 sts.)*
Work in St st for 7 rows, ending with a p row.
Inc 1 st at each end of next row. *(24 sts.)*
Work even until work measures 7in/18cm from cast-on edge, ending with a p row.
Dec 1 st at each end of next 8 rows, ending with a p row. *(8 sts.)*
Bind off.

UNDERSIDE OF BODY
Make exactly as for top of body.

EARS (MAKE 2)
With size 6 (4mm) needles and MC, cast on 6 sts.
1st row (RS) K to end.
2nd row P to end.
3rd row K2tog, k2, k2tog. *(4 sts.)*
4th row [P2tog] twice.
5th row K2tog, break off MC, thread tail end through rem st, and pull to fasten off.
Make second ear in same way.

GUINEA PIG'S COAT
With size 8 (5mm) needles and B, cast on 36 sts.
1st–4th rows K to end.
Work ³/₄in/2cm loop stitches (see page 13) on next row as follows:
5th row (WS) Place first finger of left hand behind first st on left needle, then wrap yarn around this finger and right needle at same time and k first st, do not drop st off left needle but slip st on right needle back onto left needle while keeping finger inside loop, k2tog tbl (to work slipped st and next st on left needle tog) and slide finger out of loop to complete first loop st, *wrapping yarn around first finger of left hand as before to create a loop, knit next st without dropping st from left needle, slip st just made back onto left needle and k2tog tbl; rep from * to end. *(36 sts.)*
6th row K each st tbl.
Rep 1st–6th rows 3 times more.
Knit 1 row.
Next row Cast on 6 sts onto left needle, k to end.
Rep last row once more.
Bind off knitwise.

TO FINISH
Very lightly press top and underside of body on wrong side, following instructions on yarn label. Do not press coat. With right sides together, sew top of body to underside of body, leaving a small opening. Turn right side out and insert toy filling until guinea pig is firmly filled. Sew opening closed. Sew one side edge of each ear to head as shown. (**Note:** If desired, position seam along center back of toy.)

Nose, mouth, feet, and eyes
Using A (or scrap of black yarn), embroider nose and mouth as shown. Using A, embroider feet on underside of body as shown (**Fig 1**). Sew on buttons for eyes.

Coat
Sew two ends of coat bound-off row together. Slip coat over guinea pig's head.

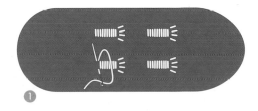
①

TORTOISE

LEVEL

Intermediate

SIZE

The finished tortoise measures approximately 6½in/16.5cm long from mouth to tip of tail and 5¼in/13.5cm wide across back legs.

MATERIALS

1 x 1¾oz/50g ball of Jaeger *Matchmaker Merino 4-Ply* in main color **MC**, for tortoise's body
1 x 1¾oz/50g ball of Rowan *Pure Wool DK* in a contrasting color **A**, for tortoise's shell
Pair of size 6 (4mm) knitting needles
Pair of size 3 (3.25mm) knitting needles
Cable needle
Toy filling

GAUGE

Tortoise's body: 28 sts and 36 rows to 4in/10cm measured over St st using size 3 (3.25mm) needles and MC.
Tortoise's shell: 22 sts and 30 rows to 4in/10cm measured over St st using size 6 (4mm) needles and A.

ABBREVIATIONS

T4LF (twist 4 left) = slip next st onto cable needle and hold at front of work, p3, then k1 from cable needle.
T4RB (twist 4 right) = slip next 3 sts onto cable needle and hold at back of work, k1, then p3 from cable needle.
Also see page 17.

TORTOISE'S BODY

The top and bottom of the tortoise's body are worked in one piece in St st, starting at the tail of the top of the body.

Shape tail
With size 3 (3.25mm) needles and MC, cast on 1 st.
1st row (RS) K into front and back of st. *(2 sts.)*
2nd row P to end.
3rd row K into front and back of each st. *(4 sts.)*
4th row P to end.

Cont in St st throughout and beg with a k row, inc 1 st at each end of next 5 rows, ending with a k row. *(14 sts.)*
Purl 1 row.

Shape back legs
Cast on 12 sts at beg of next 2 rows. *(38 sts.)*
Work even for 5 rows, ending with a k row.
Bind off 8 sts at beg of next 2 rows. *(22 sts.)*
Work even for 18 rows, ending with a k row.

Shape front legs
Cast on 8 sts at beg of next 2 rows. *(38 sts.)*
Work even for 5 rows, ending with a p row.
Bind off 12 sts at beg of next 2 rows. *(14 sts.)*

Shape neck and head
Next row (RS) [K2tog, k2] 3 times, k2tog. *(10 sts.)*
Purl 1 row.
Next row (RS) K2tog, k6, k2tog. *(8 sts.)*
Purl 1 row.

Inc 1 st at each end of next row. *(10 sts.)*
Work even for 3 rows, ending with a
p row.
**Dec 1 st at each end of next row.
Work even for 1 row.**
Rep from ** to ** once, ending with a
p row. *(6 sts.)*
Next row (RS) P to end, to create ridge
for mouth.
This completes top of tortoise's body.
Work bottom of tortoise's body as follows:

Shape neck and head
Purl 1 row.
Beg with a k row and cont in St st, inc
1 st at each end of next row. *(8 sts.)*
Purl 1 row.
Inc 1 st at each end of next row. *(10 sts.)*
Work even for 3 rows, ending with
a p row.
Dec 1 st at each end of next row. *(8 sts.)*
Purl 1 row.
Inc 1 st at each end of next row. *(10 sts.)*
Purl 1 row.
Next row (RS) K into front and back of
first st, [k2, k into front and back of next st]
3 times. *(14 sts.)*

Shape front legs
Cast on 12 sts at beg of next 2 rows.
(38 sts.)
Work even for 5 rows, ending with a
p row.
Bind off 8 sts at beg of next 2 rows.
(22 sts.)
Work even for 19 rows, ending with a
k row.

Shape back legs
Cast on 8 sts, at beg of next 2 rows.
(38 sts.)
Work even for 5 rows, ending with a
p row.
Bind off 12 sts at beg of next 2 rows.
(14 sts.)

Shape tail
Dec 1 st at each end of next row and then
at each end of 5 foll alt rows, ending with
a k row. *(2 sts.)*
Next row (WS) P2tog, then break off A,
thread tail end through rem st, and pull to
fasten off.

TOP OF TORTOISE'S SHELL
The top of the tortoise's shell is worked
starting at the neck end.
With size 6 (4mm) needles and A, cast on
26 sts.
Work 2 rows in garter st (knit every row).
Work turtle check patt as follows:
1st row (RS) K4, p6, k6, p6, k4.
2nd row P4, k6, p6, k6, p4.
3rd row K3, T4LF, T4RB, k4, T4LF,
T4RB, k3.
4th row P3, k3, p2, k3, p4, k3, p2,
k3, p3.
5th row K2, [T4LF, k2, T4RB, k2] twice.
6th row P2, [k3, p4, k3, p2] twice.
7th row K1, [T4LF, k4, T4RB] twice, k1.
8th row (inc row) K into front and back
of first st, k3, p6, k6, p6, k3, k into front
and back of last st. *(28 sts.)*
9th row P5, k6, p6, k6, p5.
10th row (inc row) K into front and back
of first st, k4, p6, k6, p6, k4, k into front
and back of last st. *(30 sts.)*
11th row [P6, k6] twice, p6.
12th row [K6, p6] twice, k6.
13th row K3, [T4RB, k4, T4LF] twice, k3.
14th row (inc row) P into front and back
of first st, p3, [k3, p4, k3, p2] twice, p1,
p into front and back of last st. *(32 sts.)*
15th row K5, [T4RB, k2, T4LF, k2] twice, k3.
16th row P6, k3, p2, k3, p4, k3, p2,
k3, p6.
17th row K6, T4RB, T4LF, k4, T4RB,
T4LF, k6.
18th row P7, k6, p6, k6, p7.
19th row K7, p6, k6, p6, k7.
20th and 21st rows Rep 18th and
19th rows.
22nd row Rep 20th row.
23rd row K6, T4LF, T4RB, k4, T4LF,
T4RB, k6.
24th row P6, k3, p2, k3, p4, k3,
p2, k3, p6.
25th row K5, [T4LF, k2, T4RB, k2]
twice, k3.
26th row P5, [k3, p4, k3, p2] twice, p3.
27th row K4, [T4LF, k4, T4RB] twice, k4.
28th row (inc row) K into front and
back of first st, [k6, p6] twice, k6,
k into front and back of last st. *(34 sts.)*
29th row P8, k6, p6, k6, p8.
30th row (inc row) K into front and
back of first st, k7, p6, k6, p6, k7,
k into front and back of last st. *(36 sts.)*

31st row P9, k6, p6, k6, p9.
32nd row K9, p6, k6, p6, k9.
33rd row Bind off first 6 sts knitwise,
k to end. *(30 sts.)*
34th row Rep 33rd row. *(24 sts.)*
K 1 row.
Bind off knitwise.

UNDERSIDE OF TORTOISE'S SHELL
The underside of the tortoise's shell is
worked starting at the tail end of the shell.
With size 6 (4mm) needles and A, cast on
20 sts.
Work 22 rows in garter st.

Shape legholes
Cont in garter st throughout, bind off 4 sts
at beg of next 2 rows.
Work even for 6 rows.
Bind off.

TO FINISH
Do not press.

Body
Fold tortoise's body in half at ridge row
(mouth), with right sides together. Sew
seam around edge of body, leaving an
opening in seam between two legs on one
side of body. Turn tortoise right side out.
Insert toy filling—do not overstuff, as the
tortoise should be fairly flat and floppy.
Sew opening closed.

Eyes
For each of tortoise's eyes, work two short
stitches on top of each other using A.

Shell
Lay shell top wrong side up and place
underside of shell right side up on top
of it; position underside so that its cast-on
edge is about 3/4in/2cm from bound-off
edge of shell top. Pin underside in place
so that shell top will create a 1/2in/12mm
overhang over it along side edges and a
1/4in/6mm overhang at shoulders. Sew
two corners on bound-off edge of
underside to shell top to form shoulders,
leaving an opening for tortoise's head.
Starting at cast on end of underside, sew
sides of underside to shell top, leaving last
6 rows of underside open for tortoise's front
legs. Pop tortoise inside its shell.

CHARTS

Carrot Curtain
(page 29)

KEY
■ p on RS and k on
  WS, using **MC**
■ k on RS and p on
  WS, using **A**

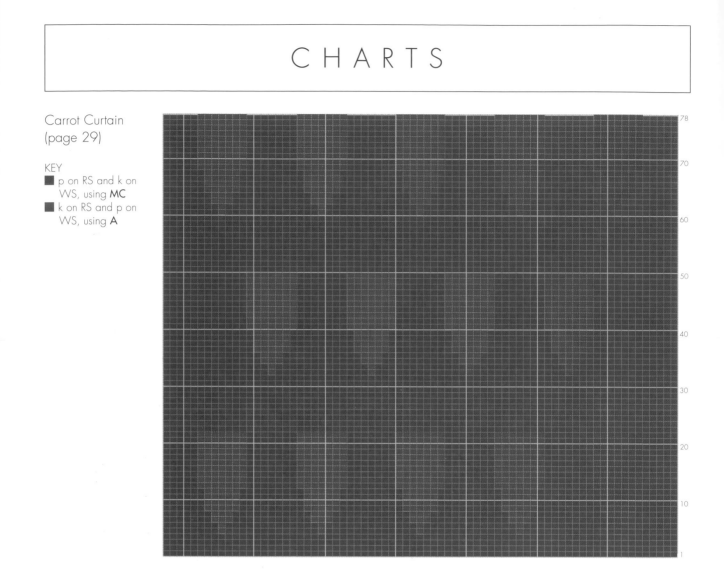

Soccer **Dog** Coat—Number
(page 33/34)

Soccer **Dog** Coat—Badge
(page 34)

KEY
■ MC
□ A

Spot **Dog** Coat (page 39)

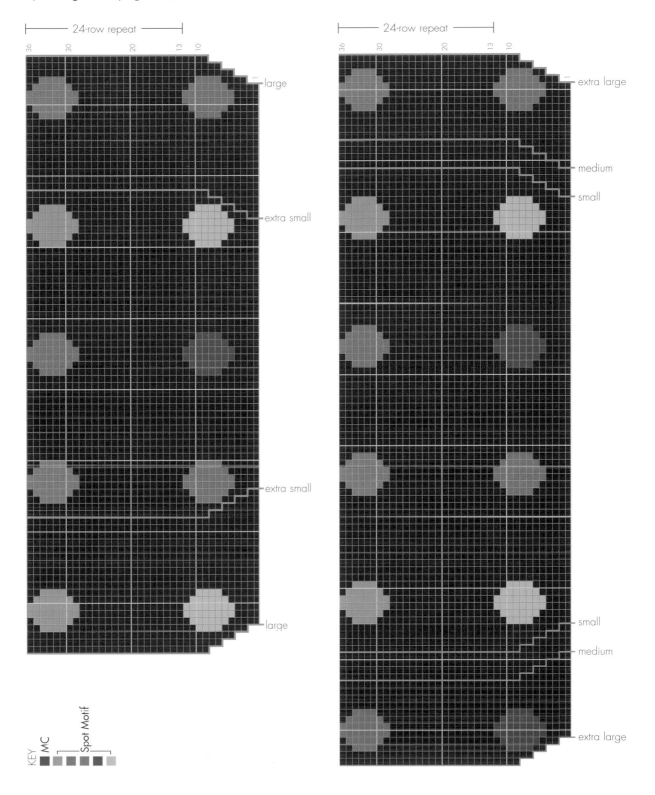

24-row repeat

36 30 20 13 10

— large

— extra small

— extra small

— large

24-row repeat

36 30 20 13 10

— extra large

— medium

— small

— small

— medium

— extra large

KEY
MC
Spot Motif

Floral **Dog** Coat
(page 42)

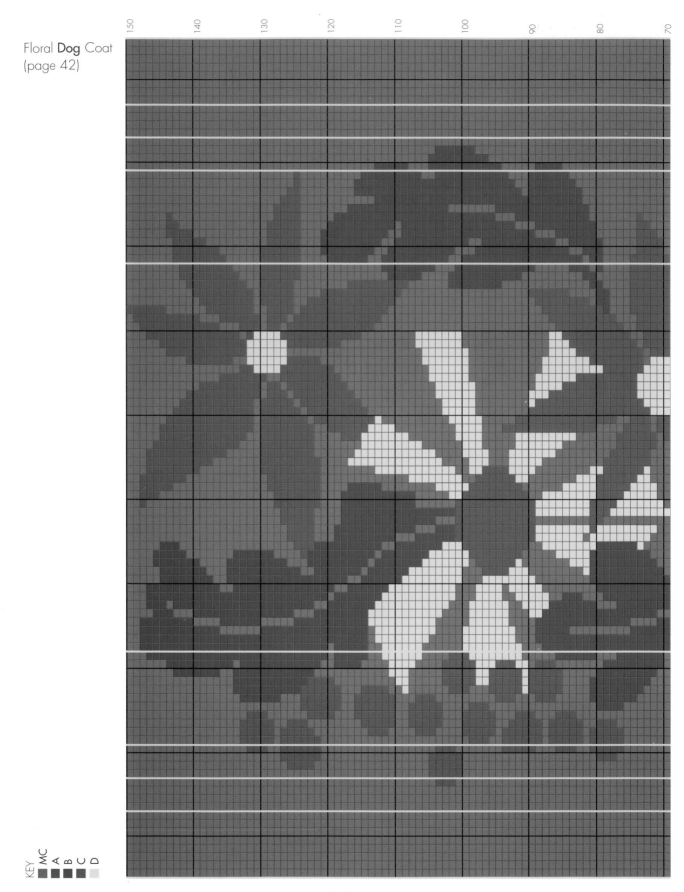

KEY
MC
A
B
C
D

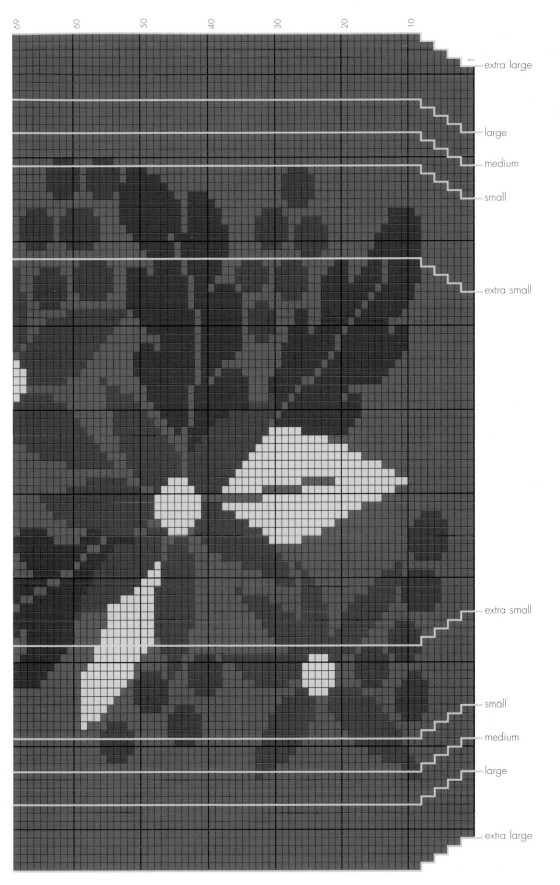

Baroque **Cat** Cushion
(page 47)

KEY
⬜ MC
⬛ A

Heraldic **Cat** Cushion
(page 49)

KEY

■ MC
■ A
■ B
■ C

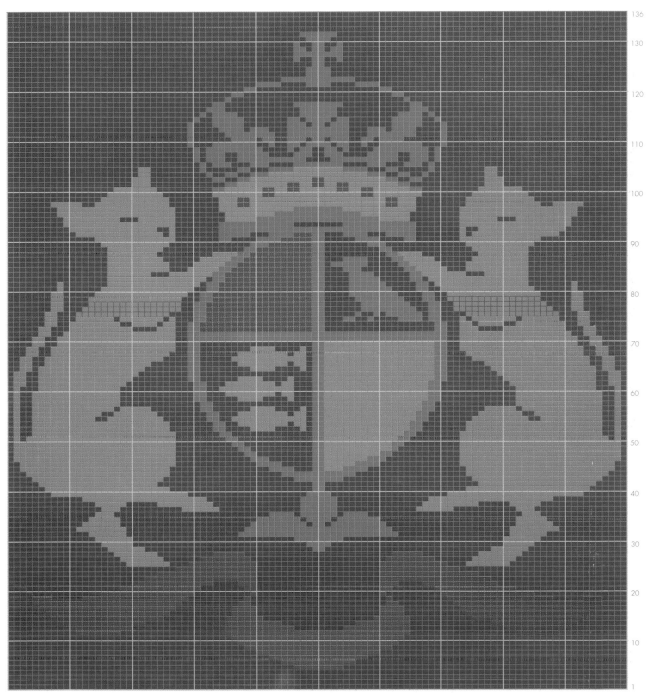

Horse Blanket—Square 1
(page 56)

KEY

■ M
■ E

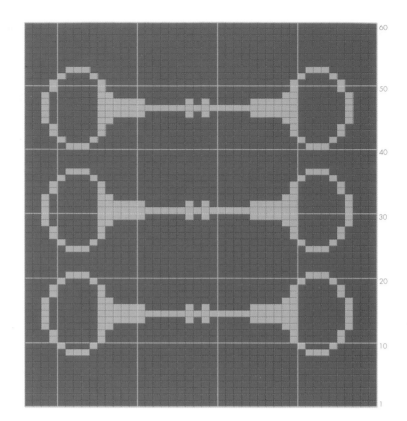

Horse Blanket—Square 3
(page 56)

KEY

■ D
■ L

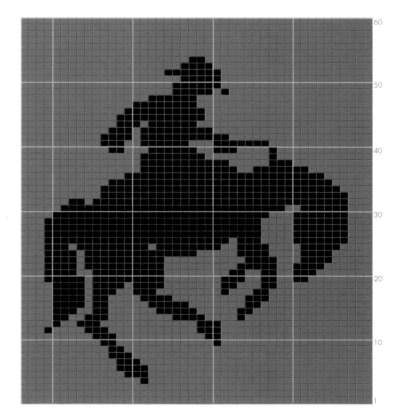

Horse Blanket—Square 6
(page 57)

KEY

■ A
■ C

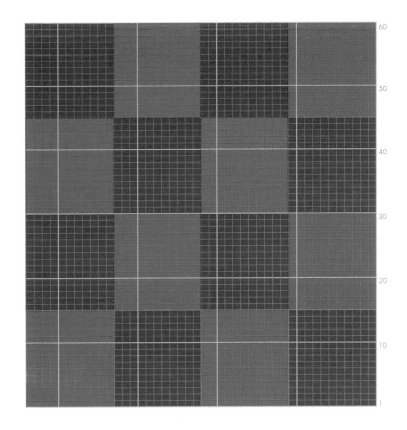

Horse Blanket—Square 8
(page 57)

KEY

■ G
☐ J
■ L

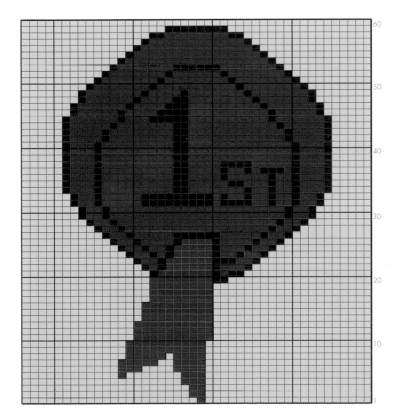

Horse Blanket—Square 9
(page 57)

KEY

■ A
■ K

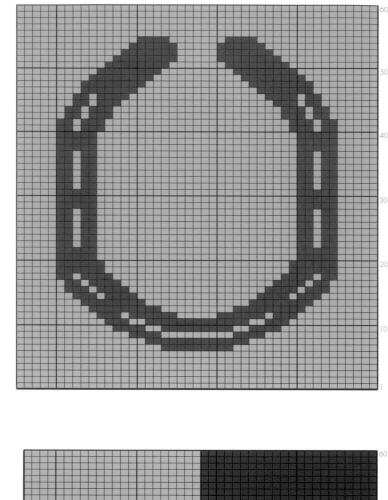

Horse Blanket—Square 14
(page 57)

KEY

■ G
■ K

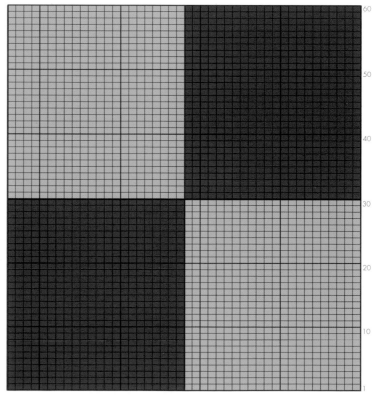

Horse Blanket—Square 15
(page 57)

KEY
■ J
■ L

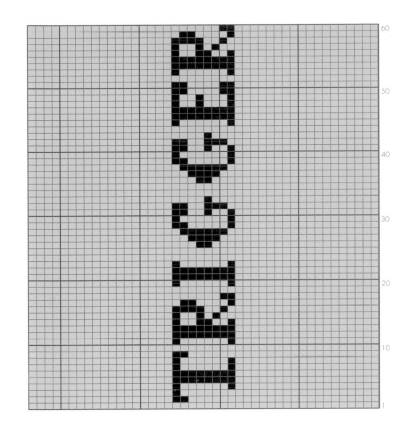

Horse Blanket—Square 17
(page 57)

KEY
■ G
■ H

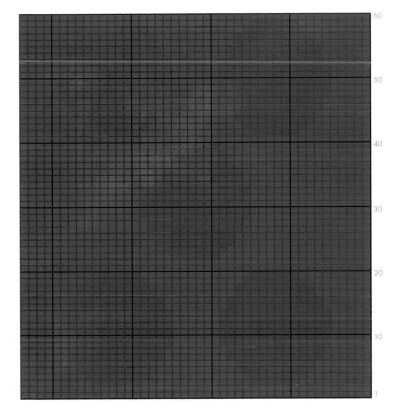

Spot **Dog** Collar
(page 67)

KEY
☐ MC
■ Spot Motif

Hell's Angel **Dog** Collar
(page 68)

KEY
■ MC
■ A
☐ B
■ C

Floral **Dog** Collar
(page 66)

KEY
■ MC
■ A
■ B
■ C
■ D

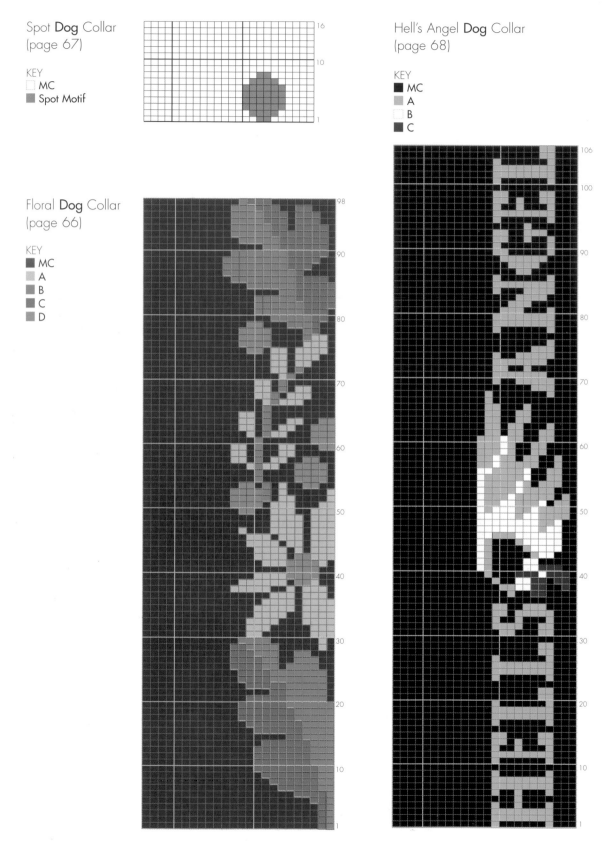

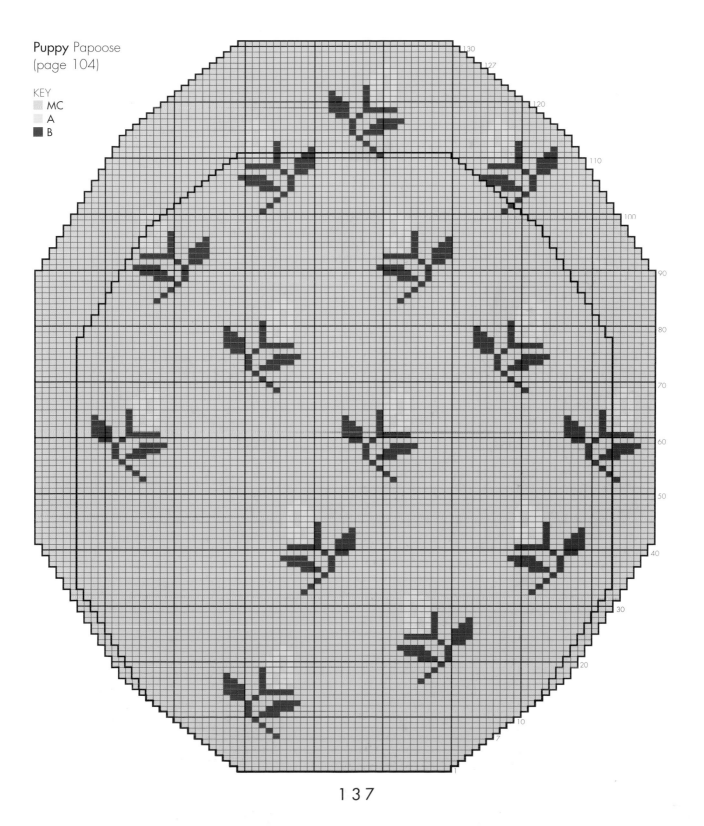

Puppy Papoose
(page 104)

KEY
MC
A
B

137

Parakeet Blanket
(page 85)

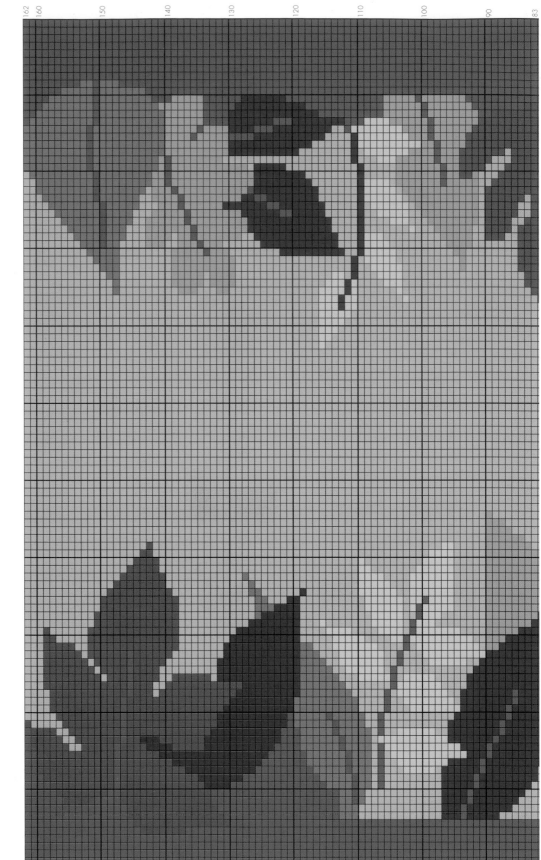

162 160 150 140 130 120 110 100 90 83

KEY
MC A B C D E F

82 80 70 60 50 40 30 20 10 1

139

Alphabet

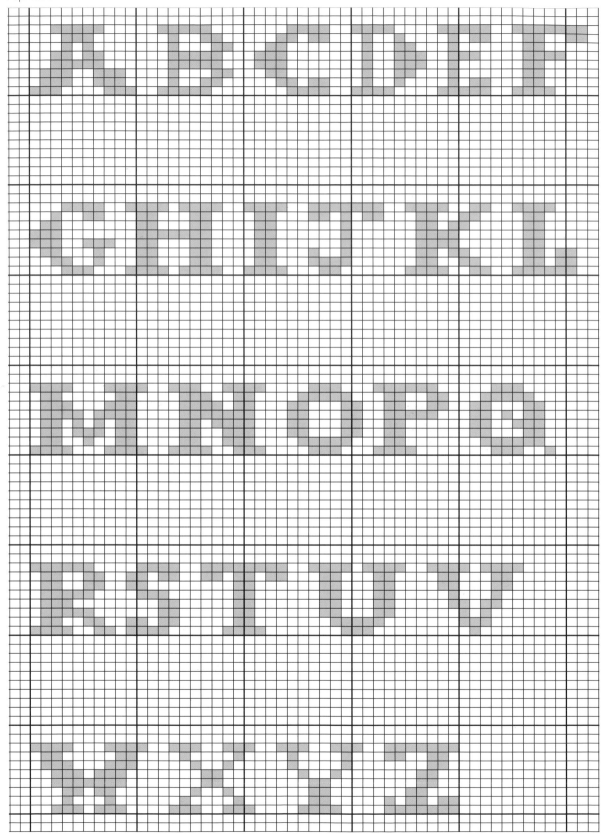

Dog Silhouettes

YARN INFORMATION

The yarns used in this book are listed here. Yarn manufacturers change their yarn colors often, so we cannot guarantee that the yarn colors specified in some of the patterns will still be available when you come to use this book. Similar shades can be used instead, or you can use your leftover yarns in your chosen color combinations.

If you wish to use a substitute yarn, be sure to look for a yarn that is similar in weight and texture, and calculate the amount you need by the length of the ball rather than by the weight. The descriptions given here for the yarns will help you identify a similar yarn for substitution.

To obtain Rowan yarns, go to the website below to find a mail-order supplier or store in your area:
www.knitrowan.com

ROWAN YARNS

Rowan *Cotton Glace*
A fine-weight 100% cotton yarn
Recommended gauge: 23 sts and 32 rows to 4in/10cm measured over St st using size 3–5 (3.25–3.75mm) knitting needles
Ball size: Approximately 126yd/115m per 1³/₄oz/50g ball

Rowan *Felted Tweed*
A lightweight wool-mix yarn
Yarn specification: 50% merino wool, 25% alpaca, 25% viscose
Recommended gauge: 22–24 sts and 30–32 rows to 4in/10cm measured over St st using size 5–6 (3.75–4mm) knitting needles
Ball size: Approximately 191yd/175m per 1³/₄oz/50g ball

Rowan *4-Ply Soft*
A super-fine-weight 100% merino wool yarn
Recommended gauge: 28 sts and 36 rows to 4in/10cm measured over St st using size 3 (3.25mm) knitting needles
Ball size: Approximately 191yd/175m per 1³/₄oz/50g ball

Rowan *Kid Classic*
A medium-weight mohair-mix yarn
Yarn specification: 70% lambswool, 26% kid mohair, 4% nylon
Recommended gauge: 18–19 sts and 23–25 rows to 4in/10cm measured over St st using size 8–9 (5–5.5mm) knitting needles
Ball size: Approximately 153yd/140m per 1³/₄oz/50g ball

Rowan *Kidsilk Haze*
A fine-weight mohair-silk-mix yarn
Yarn specification: 70% super kid mohair, 30% silk
Recommended gauge: 18–25 sts and 23–34 rows to 4in/10cm measured over St st using size 3–8 (3.25–5mm) knitting needles
Ball size: Approximately 229yd/210m per 7/8oz/25g ball

Rowan *Pure Wool DK*
A lightweight 100% super-wash wool yarn
Recommended gauge: 22 sts and 30 rows to 4in/10cm measured over St st using 6 (4mm) knitting needles
Ball size: Approximately 137yd/125m per 1³/₄oz/50g ball

Rowan *Scottish Tweed Aran*
A medium-weight 100% pure wool yarn
Recommended gauge: 16 sts and 23 rows to 4in/10cm measured over St st using size 8–9 (5–5.5mm) knitting needles
Ball size: Approximately 186yd/170m per 3¹/₂oz/100g ball

Rowan *Scottish Tweed Chunky*
A bulky-weight 100% pure wool yarn
Recommended gauge: 12 sts and 16 rows to 4in/10cm measured over St st using size 11 (8mm) knitting needles
Ball size: Approximately 109yd/100m per 3¹/₂oz/100g ball

Rowan *Scottish Tweed 4-Ply*
A fine-weight 100% pure wool yarn
Recommended gauge: 26–28 sts and 38–40 rows to 4in/10cm measured over St st using size 3 (3–3.25mm) knitting needles
Ball size: Approximately 120yd/110m per 7/8oz/25g ball

JAEGER YARNS

Jaeger *Fur*
A super-bulky-weight mohair-mix yarn
Yarn specification: 47% kid mohair, 47% wool, 6% polymide
Recommended gauge: 8 sts and 9 rows to 4in/10cm measured over St st using size 15 (10mm) knitting needles
Ball size: Approximately 22yd/20m per 1³/₄oz/50g ball

Jaeger *Matchmaker Merino DK*
A lightweight 100% merino wool yarn (machine washable)
Recommended gauge: 22 sts and 30 rows to 4in/10cm measured over St st using size 6 (4mm) knitting needles
Ball size: Approximately 131yd/120m per 1³/₄oz/50g ball

Jaeger *Matchmaker Merino 4-Ply*
A super-fine-weight 100% merino wool yarn (machine washable)
Recommended gauge: 28 sts and 36 rows to 4in/10cm measured over St st using size 3 (3.25mm) knitting needles
Ball size: Approximately 200yd/183m per 1³/₄oz/50g ball

TWILLEYS YARNS

Twilleys *Goldfingering*
A super-fine-weight metallic-mix yarn
Yarn specification: 80% viscose, 20% metallized polyester
Recommended gauge: 28 sts and 36 rows to 4in/10cm measured over St st using size 3 (3–3.25mm) knitting needles
Ball size: Approximately 108yd/100m per 7/8oz/25g ball

SUPPLIERS

Most of the materials used in this book are available from good local craft stores or try:

Creative Beadcraft
20 Beak Street
London
W1F 9RE
Tel 44 (0)20 7777629 9964
Mail order 44 (0)1494 778818
www.creativebeadcraft.co.uk

John Lewis
Oxford Street
London W1A 1EX
Tel 020 7629 7711
www.johnlewis.com

Polystyrene balls for the beanbag filling and pillow forms for cat cushions.

MacCulloch & Wallis
25–26 Dering Street
London
W1S 1AT
Tel 020 7629 0311
www.macculloch-wallis.co.uk

Calico for the beanbag cushion, striped mattress ticking and polyester satin ribbon 2in/5cm wide for the Puppy Papoose.

Muir and Osborne
33 Sillwood Road
Brighton
BN1 2LE
England
Tel + 44 (0)1273736106
www.petheaven.org.uk

Some of the accessories are available ready-made through our website.

The Bead Shop
21a Tower Street
London
WC2H 9NS
Tel 44 (0)20 7240 0931
Mail order 44 (0)20 8553 3240
www.beadshop.co.uk

Shops and mail order in America trading under "Beadworks."

The Bead Shop
21 Sydney Street
Brighton
BN1 4EN
Tel 44 (0)1273 675077
Mail order 44 (0)1273 740777
www.beadsunlimited.co.uk

Sew-on jewels for Eco-Dog Coats, fake pearls, or any beads.

ACKNOWLEDGMENTS

A book like this cannot happen overnight; we have been working on it for many months. We would like to thank our friends and families: Orlando, Daniel, Milo, Geoffrey, Abigail, Gabriel. They have all been extremely helpful both with suggestions and with tactful reactions to our ideas.

We would also like to thank all our dogs past and present who have been highly involved in our knitwear business: Alice, Fanny, Dorothy, Jack Swan, Nell, and Lily. Nell, a lovely whippet lurcher, has been the house model for the dog coats and Lily has helped in her own way.

Our wonderful and expert knitters who have worked on the patterns and tolerate demands most people wouldn't: Mrs Allday, Karen Cleverley, Kay Jones, Rosemary Moore, Mrs Saunders, Sheila Self, Jennifer Smith, Sylvia Smith, Norma Stent, Pauline Taylor, Sheila Taylor, Eileen Trudgeon, and Paula, and the Stitch and Bitch group in Frome. We must also mention all the other people, who over many years have supported us with their magnificent knitting.

Thank you to Rowan Yarns for their generosity. We are extremely grateful for the meticulous pattern checking by Marilyn Wilson and Sally Harding. Many thanks to Caroline Dawnay and Jean Edelstein for all their encouragement, and for putting us together with Quadrille.

Enormous gratitude to Jane O'Shea, Laura Herring, Katherine Case, Helen Lewis, and everyone at Quadrille, who have worked with such enthusiasm on this book and who put us together with the brilliant Diana Miller—her photographs have exceeded all our expectations.

A big thank you to all the models and animals who helped in the making of this book:

Biddy
Big Red
Charlie, the spaniel
Charlie, the terrier
Dave
Dolly and Edith
Feisty
Fred
Georgie
Grace
Ho Chi
Jake
Joey
Katie
Larry
Lila
Lily, the whippet
Lily and Gus, the pugs
Loulou
Matthew
Mooli
Mr. Q

Mrs. Mimsy
Nell
Neville
Oristano
Patch
Reggie
Ronnie
Rufus
Saint Godegrand
Sydney
Taz
Violet
Wilf

With thanks to Milton Harries for the race horses.

Many thanks to Hackney City Farm.

And in loving memory of Sandy and Burt, R.I.P.